GUIDES
guardians
AND
angels

D. J. CONWAY

ENHANCE RELATIONSHIPS WITH YOUR SPIRITUAL COMPANIONS

GUIDES

guardians

⟨ AND ⟩

angels

Llewellyn Publications
Woodbury, Minnesota

First Edition
First Printing, 2009

Book design by Steffani Sawyer
Book edited by Brett Fechheimer
Cover art © 2009 PhotoDisc
Cover design by Ellen Dahl
Interior illustrations by the Llewellyn Art Department
Llewellyn is a registered trademark of Llewellyn Worldwide, Ltd.

Library of Congress Cataloging-in-Publication Data

Conway, D. J. (Deanna J.).
    Guides, guardians and angels : enhance relationships with your
spiritual companions / Deanna J. Conway. — 1st ed.
       p. cm.
    Includes bibliographical references.
    ISBN 978-0-7387-1124-9
    1. Guides (Spiritualism) 2. Guardian angels. 3. Angels. I. Title.
    BF1275.G85C66 2009
    133.9—dc22
                                          2008042763

Llewellyn Publications
A Division of Llewellyn Worldwide, Ltd.
2143 Wooddale Drive, Dept. 978-07387-1124-9
Woodbury, Minnesota 55125-2989, U.S.A.
www.llewellyn.com

Printed in the United States of America

Other Books by D. J. Conway

Animal Magick
By Oak, Ash, & Thorn
Celtic Magic
Dancing with Dragons
Magickal Mystical Creatures
Mystical Dragon Magick

To my brother Harvey and my friend Ray Page,
who refused to let me give up.

Contents

CONTENTS

1. INTRODUCTION

Guides, guardians, and angels. Are they the same beings? Some-times. Can they perform the same functions? Not always. Are they available to all humans, even those who don't believe in them? Absolutely. They believe in us even if we don't believe in them.

Many books have been written on these three classes of astral beings, and none of these books is necessarily wrong. However, from the number of questions I'm asked all the time, it seems that many people still don't understand these beings, especially angels. Although I hope to add a few more facts and thoughts to these subjects, I don't consider this book to be the last word on the information either. New facts and knowledge will inevitably appear in the future as humans progress spiritually.

Humans tend to look upon guides, guardians, and especially angels as fluffy cloud entities that are never critical or tough with us. Surprise! These beings have specific jobs to do. Either they accept the rough, complicated task of helping humans, who usually ignore their advice and help, or they have strict, regimented jobs of helping humans and keeping everything concerning humans on a path that follows the laws of the Goddess and the God. Some of these beings perform their tasks with compassion, but little emotion. Others show emotions easily. All three classes of entities can appear, if necessary, very harsh in their correction and teaching of humans. Since we stubborn humans resist change, our astral helpers have to be strict.

Originally, I had no intention of writing about these subjects. I knew there were glaring errors out there about angels, but I'm not a professional translator. I needed resource material to collaborate my own findings. In the mid-1990s, books by Professor Elaine Pagels and other noted translators became available. These books revealed and corrected the information about angels. Nearly all these translations from the original languages and texts agreed with my research and intuitive interpretations. This new way of thinking about angels made me reappraise two other categories of spiritual beings that work with humans: spirit guides and guardians.

I've written a little on guides and guardians before, but not all that I know about them. People frequently misunderstand, or are confused about, guides and guardians as well as angels.

After all, every writer has his or her own spin on these topics. By the time I finished researching all these subjects, tracing threads of their existence back through religious and secular histories, I felt I wanted to share this reconstructed information. I considered it important that readers learn how to work with these spiritual beings in a practical way. So I decided that a book on guides, guardians, and real angels seemed appropriate at this time.

I imagine there will be people who disagree with my findings. Not everyone views such abstract ideas in the same way. When it comes to abstract ideas, particularly those dealing with the spiritual, people tend to be overly sensitive to information that doesn't express their personal views. Examples are the persecutions of some of history's greatest thinkers who insisted that the earth was round, not flat, and that the earth moved around the sun, not vice versa. We should always be prepared to view new information with the idea that our personal opinions were formed without knowing all the facts. It doesn't mean we will change our opinions, for the new "facts" may not be the entire truth just yet. But we should always be willing to learn and adjust our thinking where necessary. During my research, I had to change some views I had on certain subjects that I cover in this book. When I revised my opinions, I discovered helpful, new ways of working with these beings.

In this book I will describe each class of being as I have experienced it. I also will offer several guided meditations and rituals to help you form friendships and working connections with these important entities. The more you work with these astral beings, the closer you will become to them. The closer you become, the more you will be aware of their presence and be open to their advice.

Guides, guardians, and angels are powerful, important beings that influence human lives. Rather than ignore their existence or their power to make our lives better, we need to reconnect with each class of entity. If our telepathic networks of communications with them are smooth, we will not have to struggle so much when we need their help. Our acceptance of, and work with, guides, guardians, and angels allows them to fulfill their appointed objectives of spiritually aiding humans. They also help us as we work on our personal goals in this lifetime.

Rather than break into a train of thought in later chapters, and have to footnote, I've included a few basics in the appendix at the end of the book. Although such things as chakras and auras may be common knowledge to many readers, others may not be familiar with this field of study at all. The same applies to the Otherworld and its layout. You will be using some of each technique to build a communicating link with the spirit beings you will read about in this book.

For those of you who are skeptical about your abilities to communicate with these Otherworld beings, please consider this beautiful quote from Helen Keller, the blind and deaf woman who overcame extreme challenges to experience life in all its facets: "The best and most beautiful things in the world cannot be seen or even touched. They must be felt with the heart."

Also, open your minds to the intelligent, open-minded voices of the past who made the following statements about spiritual paths:

What is food to one man may be fierce poison to another.
—LUCRETIUS (C. 95–55 BCE)

One religion is as true as another.
—ROBERT BURTON (1577–1640)

*There are nine and sixty ways of constructing tribal lays,
and every single one of them is right!*
—RUDYARD KIPLING (1865–1936)

One man's god is another man's devil.
—UNKNOWN

All goddesses and gods are One, and the One is All.
—ANGELS' SONG IN 2002

In other words, there is no "one and only way" to look at something, particularly spiritual beliefs.

2. GUIDES

History of Guides

Cultures around the world have an extremely long history of believing in and working with spirit guides. The names used by different cultures are frequently not the same, but the premises and descriptions behind the spiritual ideas are. The best-known guide mentioned in Greek history is the daemon who accompanied Socrates, who called it a being that spoke to him in an inner voice. A daemon isn't a demon, although many people who believe only in what they can see and touch believe this to be the case. I find this attitude amazing because the same scoffers believe in bacteria, atoms, and tachyons. What Socrates described was clearly his spiritual guide.

Long before the beginning of recorded Celtic history, the Celtic clans believed that each person had an *anam cara* that gave them advice. Later, *anam cara* came to mean both a spiritual being or a close human friend. However, the intent of the anam cara, whether spirit or human, remained the same—spiritual advice for everyday life.

Types of Guides and Meditations

At least one spiritual guide comes in with each person when that person is born and remains with that person until they leave the physical body, in what we call "death." This spiritual guide is available at all times, if we take the time to listen. Although you will always have this one main guide, other guides may appear to help teach you certain topics necessary for your overall development. These additional guides may become life companions, coming and going on a schedule of their own. Or they may merely do their job, and you will never see them again.

Your main guide may not be similar to you in race or culture. Your guide may not be what you expect at all. When it comes to spiritual guides, what we think we want may not be what we need and get.

Many people make the mistake of wishing for a soul mate as a guide, as well as a companion in life. The modern meaning of the term *soul mate* has been twisted to mean a wonderful, no-problems-ever person who will enrich the joy in your life; actually, this meaning should be applied instead to the term *other half of your heart*. A soul mate usually has no sexual or marital connotations. The relationship, which can be either good or bad, has an unconditional, tight bond built through thousands of years. This can be a family member, a friend, or someone you meet only for a brief period of time. This bond can be built on strong attractions or equally strong differences. A soul mate comes into your life to make you learn a needed lesson. Unfortunately, most of the soul-mate lessons are painful ones. Why? Because humans seem to remember the results of painful decisions longer than decisions that are not painful.

A spirit guide is not necessarily one that has been with you in previous lifetimes, but is likely one that chooses (or is chosen) to work with you when you agree to reincarnate. Although we all have free will about reincarnating, sometimes we are given a push to do so because we need more earthly training. The guide reviews all your past lives to detect any weak areas that need to be strengthened, your strong areas that could benefit the people you will meet in the new incarnation, and the parts of your individual personality that persist from lifetime to lifetime. In other words, the guide tries to understand and know you as much as possible so that the relationship will be a productive one. The guide hopes to learn from this experience as much as you do.

Spirit guides, with the help of Master Teachers, personally tailor the lessons they want to teach their human students. If necessary, they will give you the same lesson in several guises until you get it. Then they build the next lessons on the foundation of the previous ones. Each lesson also has interior, mini-lessons that affect the student (you) on the physical, mental, emotional, and spiritual levels. Your personal spirit guide tries to pack as much information and training as possible into the time you give them. Plus, your guide will help you with your personal life as much as possible. They have active, full schedules for your entire lifetime. If we would listen more, all involved would have an easier time.

Since your guide works with you for some time before you are reborn into an earthly life, your guide cannot be anyone who was alive when you were born. The spiritual being must also undergo training to become a qualified guide. So if you detect deceased family members or friends around you, they are there to comfort and help you if possible. But such a family member is not your true spiritual guide—not unless he or she is a very distant relative.

A word of caution here: If you didn't get along with certain family members or other people when they were alive, do not expect that they will have changed their personality and traits just because they died. If they criticized, humiliated, or made fun of you before, it is highly likely they will continue to do so, if you let them. However, you have the right to demand that these unwanted spirits not be allowed around you, and they will have to leave.

It is up to each person to decide about the type of spiritual company and guides he or she wants. Any spirit, even a deceased relative or friend, who skirted the law when alive, or who was devious, critical, humiliating, or cared little about changing for the better, will still be unreliable after physical death. Becoming a spirit doesn't change personality, ethics, or credibility. And being dead doesn't necessarily make one more intelligent. It takes a lot of determination and reincarnations to become a reliable expert in any field. So if Uncle Joe continues to whisper in your mind that you will never amount to anything, demand that he leave and never return. If any deceased people's thoughts of failure (however they defined failure) and criticism keep ringing in your head and impede you from building self-confidence, ask your guardians and angels to keep the offenders permanently away from you. Physical death simply doesn't change people's negative habits. And your allowing them to hang around, continuing their old patterns, hurts both of you.

Actually, it is best to leave deceased loved ones and friends on a friendship basis only, with occasional visits, and ask that only the highest, most positive guides available be sent to you. If you request a certain type of additional guide (such as a fairy, elf, or Native American shaman), still ask for the wisest, most positive guide.

Guides, particularly helper guides, are a widely varied group of beings that see that we learn as much truth in all areas and on all levels as possible in each lifetime. The helper guides include nature spirits, fairies, elves, devas, and sometimes power animals and even mythical creatures.

Some people make the mistake of calling their main guide a Master Teacher or Master Guide, even a guru. This is rarely accurate. It is better to use the names *primary guide* or *main guide* only. A true Master Teacher very seldom takes on the teaching of just one person. They are the Teachers of teachers, your spirit guides. They are rather like technical advisors for guides, thus working with millions of people at the same time. The Masters also bear the heavy burden of escorting souls to the Otherworld when there are wars, mass tragedies, or fatal natural disasters, which involve the loss of hundreds or thousands of lives within a short period of time.

Before you decided to be born into your present lifetime, your spirit guide helped you draw up a life plan. This plan involves what karma you want to balance, what lessons or experiences you decide to learn, and what goals you hope to accomplish. This complicated list is then figured into a matching natal chart, which must be approved by the Council and the Astra-Keepers before it is considered final. This life plan frequently includes your good intentions of being available to help certain other people learn lessons or balance karma that was written into their own life plans. Most often these good intentions involve entering a particular family, marrying unsuitable spouses, or befriending ungrateful people. Few if any of these plans work out.

We all forget our past lives, as well as our present life plans, the moment we are born. A few humans accurately remember bits and pieces of past lives, if we aren't "punished" out of such memories. It is only common sense that full memory of past lives would make existing in this lifetime an insane impossibility. Our minds and souls would be screaming "Overload!" I've often wondered if many people who are declared mentally unbalanced, and not from brain damage or other obvious reasons, are misunderstood psychic souls who can't separate this lifetime from remembered past lives. Or if their connection with the Otherworld is so strong and constant that they cannot separate the two worlds. Until psychologists and psychiatrists accept this possibility, and explore this area with open minds, we may never know for certain.

Forgetting even the highlights of our personal life plan, let alone the details, leaves us vulnerable and back to square one with each new life. The only help we have are our spirit guides who planned with us. They also have the option of petitioning the Council at any time to terminate a karmic lesson (if learned), lightening the load if it becomes too heavy, or providing more options if our actions earn that right. Spirit guides are our cheering section in life, the ones who really care the most if we succeed or fail in our missions, if we gain ground or lose it in our attempts to fulfill the life plan.

The more people involved in one of your attempts to balance karma, especially in family groups, the more likelihood of group failure. Other people involved simply won't cooperate, will refuse to forgive and let karma balance itself, or will insist on holding onto past-life grudges and hates. However, if you do your part, the rest of the group will no longer be attached to your future lives. All you can do is be respectful, according to the relationship (such as parents, siblings, and other close connections), until such time as you are on your own. Then, the best method is to put physical distance between you and to remain as respectful as possible, without being a doormat.

You learn to distinguish between true friends and false through personal experience, just as you hopefully recognize negative intimate relationship problems and break the cycle. We all have free-will choice to ignore the intuitive help from our spirit guides. We can wear blinders and keep being hurt and miserable by repeating mistakes for an entire lifetime.

Frequently, the biggest changes we need to make are within ourselves. After all, the only person you can change *is* yourself. You need to figure out why you have such an internal compulsion to keep being a victim, an abuser, a controller, a manipulator, or a doormat. When you correct these types of internal tapes, the attracting energy shifts. The troubles or troublesome people, who were always available to make your life less than desirable, vanish.

Because everyone has free will, you have no right to insist upon, or attempt to force on others, changes you feel are right. If you make fulfilling your life plan of prime importance, and try to be the best person you can be, I guarantee you will have a very busy, productive life. Anything and anyone you feel is on the wrong path should be turned over to the Goddess or the God, while you go on to better things.

One of the best communication tools available, open to anyone willing to invest some time and practice, is meditation. It helps your subconscious mind link to the limitless super-conscious mind of the Multiverse, so you can discover and implement information pertinent to your personal situation. Meditation thins the veil between this realm of existence and the Otherworld. In this manner, you develop clearer distinct links and communications with your spirit guides.

You also learn to discern spirit energies—positive or nega-tive. You can talk yourself into hearing anything you want to hear if you don't demand only the truth. And that means the truth about yourself as well as truth from spirit beings.

Once your line to your spirit guides is open, you will dis-cover you've heard them all the time. You just chose to ignore the messages or passed them off as imagination. It is extremely rare to hear the guides with your physical ears. Their connec-tion instead is a line of conversation-thoughts in your mind, with words, phrases, information, ways of thinking, even tone of voice you know aren't yours. They often reinforce these messages by exposing you repeatedly to symbols in the physi-cal world as a means of identification and verification.

For example, you wonder if you should attend a certain event or take a short vacation to a particular place. Would doing so benefit your life and career? Within a short time, sev-eral credible people mention that they met influential people at a previous such event, or that the vacation spot you're con-sidering has wonderful cultural and spiritual attractions, or a respectable business there is seeking a person with your talents. This much verification cannot be considered coincidence. Anyway, there are no coincidences—just answers and opportunities.

Your guides always answer in a multitude of ways. You simply have to be watchful and use common sense. You have to follow through on opportunities. Guides will not drop your desires in your lap, fully grown with every *t* crossed.

Although I've received an entire library of forgotten information through the years, I never take anything at face value immediately. I'm a skeptic on accepting radically new things. I think about every idea for a long time, research it if possible, weigh the information against what I already know, and of course write it down. My guides have not yet provided me with false information, even though some of their predictions didn't happen until as much as five years into the future.

As a young child, I was aware that Gray Wolf, a Native American, accompanied me everywhere, as did several Native American children. I always called him Grandfather when talking to him. It wasn't until I was an adult that I learned the past-life connection between the two of us. It was Gray Wolf who warned me about lower spirits sometimes trying to masquerade as spirit guides. And it was he who taught me a simple but effective method of preventing that from happening.

This method is an efficient, quick way to clean out all the chakras and auras, and is especially protective when done before meditations or astral travel. As a child, I didn't know anything about chakras or auras; I called them *inside lights* (chakras) and *outside lights* (auras). If you are interested in the placement and descriptions of the auras and chakras, these are given in the appendix, along with illustrations.

Cleansing Exercise

To perform this cleansing exercise, all you need is a little quiet time to sit down, close your eyes, and relax. While you take a slow, deep breath, visualize earth energy entering your body from the Earth Star chakra, which lies between your feet and is connected to the minor chakras found in the sole of each foot. This is a strong grounding energy that reenergizes all the chakras, from the feet to above the head, and the auras of the body, from the innermost to the outermost. Slowly, breathe out as this earth energy works its magick. Relax and take a normal breath. On the next breath, take another deep breath, and as you exhale this time, draw in brilliant white light. This light will swiftly clear all the chakras from top to bottom, as well as push out debris in the auras from the innermost to the outer layer. Sit for a moment longer, and let your body absorb all this power.

(End of exercise)

At the very beginning of working with my other guides and teachers, I was afraid of lower-level spirits getting in with deceptions, so I set firm rules. No lower spirits or deceased relatives with whom I didn't get along before they died were allowed near me. No possession would ever be allowed. If the positive guides didn't keep out the negative ones, I wouldn't be speaking with any of them. Since guides are of particular importance to every person, I felt I had every right to make these rules.

Guides are the one constant link we each have to the Otherworld, no matter how alone we feel in this life. They are teachers of everything from ethics and outlook on life to actual studies in astral schools and more. They come in all races, cultures, and colors, regardless of what we are. Their dress and the manner of their first appearance may upset us, depending upon our personal, private attitudes and circumstances. However, if upset or misunderstanding happens on the first contact, they will retreat to let us think about it. Then they will reappear slightly altered to a more acceptable appearance the next time. This is done not to mislead us, but to befriend us.

This happened with my first primary guide and teacher, Ramashan, from ancient Tibet. He appeared to me in a meditation just a few months after my oldest daughter died in a car accident. I was sitting in a beautiful Otherworld garden, one I recognized later as the Healing Garden of the Upperworld. I was absorbing the tranquil silence when I looked up to see a short figure in a creamy white robe, face hidden in a hood, hands covered by long sleeves, intently and silently watching me from a short distance away. I say "watching," for he was obviously doing that, although I could see nothing of his face. There was nothing dark or gruesome about him, but the meditation burst like a soap bubble. His image was not something I expected to see.

When Ramashan appeared in meditation again a few weeks later, he left behind his concealing robe. He revealed himself as the kindly monk he was, complete with a dry, wicked, down-to-earth sense of personality and a fantastic knowledge of events as far back as the arrival of the star travelers who settled Atlantis. He never minced words or skirted any delicate subject if he had something to say.

Ramashan is not quite five feet tall, but he has an air of self-assurance that makes him seem seven feet tall. His mischievous dark eyes sparkle under black brows, with a smoothly shaved head above. He assures me he could appear without the character-enhancing wrinkles but chooses not to. He once told me, "No one takes a younger person seriously about spiritual and historical matters, at least they once didn't. Today, the world is crazy." He is the wisest man I've ever met and as energetic as a newly hatched dragonfly.

Shortly after Ramashan began teaching me on very deep subjects, a series of guides arrived, all with different talents, one after another within the space of a few months. It was as if my willingness had opened a series of doors into the Otherworld.

One of these was Doctor Ch'in of herbal, stone, and color magick. I think he was as surprised as I was, and not too happy to find himself with a European, and a woman at that! He delivered his lectures in professorial tones, then disappeared for periods of time. Obviously, he had no desire to be in constant attendance. All he wanted with me was an occasional "class" to make me remember what I had learned in the past about stones, herbs, symbols, and colors.

Although many teachers come and go in my life, there is always a polite sense of order. Among the teachers who make frequent appearances are two of whom I've become quite fond: Meritaten and Pandra Shanti. Meritaten is a young woman of ancient Egypt; she wears a simple white gown, a braided black wig, and rich jewelry. I was shocked, years later, to find proof of her actual existence through her name. I now own a small replica of her original carved bust.

I once asked Meritaten why I had more men than women as teacher-guides. Her answer was that the male energy balanced my strong femininity and right-brain activities. It took Pandra Shanti's love of swords and his challenge to learn to dance with a shamshir to make me realize Meritaten was very accurate.

Pandra Shanti was the second teacher to appear, and he is the most fascinating Persian court vizier and magician I could hope to meet. His ability to laugh at his own past blunders and successes in magick delight me. Not only that, but he must have been outstanding in looks, even in his day. Well over six feet tall, with that glorious golden-brown Arabic skin, long black hair, and dark eyes heavily lined with black lashes, he would be mobbed in any modern mall. His muscular hands and fingers are long, narrow, and studded with gemstone rings; he wears silver and gold rings in his pierced ears.

He likes to wear embroidered tunics and a type of trousers with billowy legs. Over these he wears a long open-front robe covered with magickal symbols. For all this, no one would think him the least bit effeminate. He considers fancy slippers unmanly, so he tucks his trousers into calf boots of tooled leather instead. Rather than a conical hat, he wears a turban secured in front with a large ruby pin. A sharp shamshir (the Persian equivalent of a scimitar) and a couple of drawstring bags hang from his leather belt. He absolutely destroyed my stereotyped mental image of a court magician. He knows how to use that shamshir and later taught me to dance with it.

Pandra Shanti likes to be the center of attention. He was quick to tell me of his successful spells, and just as quick to make fun of his failures. However, if someone tried to pry into magickal secrets, he wasn't adverse to saying no, and noting exactly what character faults made the person not safe to have that information. He has great knowledge and power but little tact. Furthermore, he doesn't care about tact.

These meditational experiences with a variety of teachers began many years of intensive learning that only paused in 2000, when my husband was diagnosed with terminal cancer. From 2000 until his death in 2002, my guides and teachers switched to emotional support and spiritual healing. The stress of those two years took its toll; to everyone's shock I suffered a

heart attack and stroke in 2003. When the cardiologists failed
to arrange rehabilitation, Pandra Shanti and Meritaten took
matters into their own hands. Meritaten encouraged me to
learn Middle Eastern dance with a local teacher. I walked like a
drunk with a cane into that class at the end of April 2003, and
no longer used the cane before October of that year.

Pandra Shanti is a very cunning spirit guide. He encouraged me to collect swords as I could afford them. By the time
I laid aside the cane, I got the opportunity to buy a shamshir
at an unbelievable price. A shamshir is similar to a curved
scimitar but has less curve, and is heavier and balanced slightly
differently. Mine is thirty-nine inches from pommel to point,
and three inches at the widest part of the blade. It weighs five
pounds, less than the one the Persian carries.

No sooner had I gotten the sword than there was Pandra
Shanti, his fancy court robes and rings laid aside, a big smile
on his face, and his shamshir in hand. He challenged me to let
him teach me how to dance with that heavy sword. It wasn't
easy, but I learned. I even managed it without damage to fur-
niture or cats. It took quite a while to strengthen my wrists
and hands so I could swing the sword with one hand and control that swing. Even a lighter sword isn't made for a woman's
hands and muscles. But the discipline of learning this skill—
right-brain dancing and left-brain, slightly modified warrior
sword-training—taught me how to better balance energy flows
and brain activity for magickal and spiritual practices.

The reason I share these events is to show how guides don't
always teach in the ways we expect, nor may they be the type of
guides we thought we needed. They frequently work together,
as did Meritaten and Pandra Shanti, to get across a lesson and
prove a point. They cleverly challenged me with a combina-

tion of Egyptian temple dance and sword practice. The combination gives a more than adequate body and mental workout. And the muscular workout was better for me than boringly jogging on a treadmill.

The present challenge from my Persian guide is to learn to dance with two shorter swords at the same time. He assures me that the sword training will involve learning defensive moves with daggers. When I challenged his use of the word *dagger* to describe a twenty-two-inch weapon, he laughed. To a warrior his size, anything shorter than thirty inches is a belt knife for eating. Since Pandra Shanti knows he has my complete attention, I'm warily looking for the lesson that will come with this. It will undoubtedly be much more complex than the one that came with the original sword dance.

Even though I've shared my personal experiences in finding and working with spirit guides, that doesn't mean yours will be the same at all. Don't compare your psychic and spiritual experiences with those of other people. Each of us is unique. Therefore, our experiences will be unique, suited to each of us. What one person "sees" within her mind, another may "feel" within himself. The impact and the message may be the same. How we each perceive it, and what we gain from it, will not be. You should be open-minded when studying new information. Just don't be so open-minded that you lose your common sense and discernment.

It is always permissible, and wise, to ask questions until you either accept or reject (as not for you) any new path or method. Sometimes you'll find yourself in a middle ground where you can't make an informed decision at that time. That's fine too. Put the subject aside until you find that final piece of the puzzle. It may take years, but don't worry about it. I've waited nearly sixty years for proof that will solidify my opinion on one subject. In the meantime, keep learning new subjects and expanding your spiritual growth in other directions.

The easiest method for getting acquainted with your primary spirit guide, and then with other guides and teachers, is through simple meditation. Meditation is very safe; you can end it at any time. Your body will not be taken over by some wandering spirit low-life, nor will you ever lose your soul. You don't need to be with another person or a group for it to work. All it takes is patience, persistence, and practice. The wonderful thing, besides visiting the Otherworld and your guides, is that no two meditations will ever be the same.

First, you need to do a few things that will prevent your being interrupted or startled out of a meditation. Shut off the phone; a ringing phone is a terribly jarring noise. Put a "Do Not Disturb" sign on your door. If you light a white candle, be sure to put it in a fireproof holder and a safe place where it can't start a fire. You can burn incense as long as the ventilation is good and the room is not too small. You don't want the fumes to make you cough. If you have a quartz crystal or other stone you feel is special, you can hold it during the meditation.

You may want to tape the guided meditations rather than try to remember what happens next. Be sure to leave blank spaces for exploring. You will discover that, after becoming comfortable with meditation, you may not hear the tape at all until the ending. You may have wandered off to explore something not even mentioned on the tape.

The beginning of each meditation in this book will be the same. Rather than repeat this beginning, later meditations will give the page number. Study the Otherworld chart and descriptions in the appendix before you start the meditation, so you will have an idea about where you go.

Meeting Your Spirit Guide Meditation

(Beginning of meditation)

Sit in a comfortable chair, feet flat on the floor, with your hands in your lap. Cleanse your chakras and auras by the breathing technique described earlier in this chapter, on page 16. Sit quietly and let your body relax as much as possible, beginning with your feet and moving upward to your head. See yourself standing beside a well. If anything or anyone in your life is upsetting you, drop it, or them, into the well. Walk away, leaving every annoying person or event behind.

(End of beginning)

You feel very relaxed as you walk across a meadow toward a high wall covered with vining flowers. An ornate gate stands open, waiting for you. You walk through the gate and find yourself in a beautiful, expansive garden. You see all types of temples through the green trees. There are groves of trees, stone walkways, bridges over little streams, small lakes surrounded by more buildings, pools of bright fish. Everywhere are flowers, butterflies, birds, dragonflies, mythical creatures, and nonthreatening animals. In the distance these gardens gradually blend into rising hills. There is a strong feeling of peace and serenity everywhere you go.

Almost all spirit guides are found in the Middleworld of the Otherworld. This area of the Otherworld is very similar in appearance to this plane of existence, except that you may see fairies, elves, and other such beings. Colors will be more vivid also.

As you look around you, a tall stone, grove of trees, or a temple attracts your attention. You quickly move toward it, for you know inside that your primary spirit guide will meet you there. When you arrive at your destination, you see a figure waiting for you, smiling and happy to finally be recognized.

Spend as much time as you wish looking at your guide. Ask for a name, and introduce yourself. Is your guide male or female? Young or old in appearance? Can you discern a culture or nationality? If you feel uncomfortable with this guide, try to decide why. If the discomfort continues, politely ask the guide to leave and send another spirit guide. The discomfort often comes from inner prejudices or past experiences. If this is the case, you will need to work through these problems.

You and your guide are free to go anywhere in the gardens that you wish. You will find chairs and benches if you want to sit and talk. Or you may wish your guide to act as a tour guide to places that interest you. Talk about what you need to work on first in your life. Take all the time you need to get acquainted and become friends. Your spirit guide is the one friend you can always count on to be with you when you need comfort or advice.

You may meet other guides and traveling people in the gardens. Some may stop and talk a while; others may be too intent on their own discoveries to speak at this time.

When you have finished the visit for this time, simply think of your physical body. You will return at once to your body in the chair. Relax a few minutes, thinking about your experiences. You may want to write down your experiences, so you can remember them later.

(End of meditation)

You may also use the above meditation to meet more teacher-guides. After you have meditated and kept an open mind for a while, you will find that guides and teachers meet you as soon as you enter your meditation. If you send a mental invitation a little while before your meditation, you are likely to have more spirits waiting for you.

It is worthwhile to consider asking for a spirit shaman as a companion and guide through the Otherworld. It isn't necessary that you have one, but a shaman is good company when traveling during meditations. You may ask for a specific type of shaman: fairy, elf, Native American, Celtic, African, or any other cultural shaman. Personally, I prefer dragon, fairy, or elf shamans. They are the closest to nature and all nature spirits.

You may find that you meet a certain shaman on one visit, but a different one on the next visit. Frequently, they will walk with you and your spirit guide while answering your questions.

Meeting an Otherworld Shaman

(Use the cleansing method mentioned on page 16, and the meditation beginning practices listed on page 23.)

As you enter the gate to the magickal gardens, you immediately feel that there is one special area where you should go. You find a path heading in that direction. Birds, butterflies, or other creatures may go before you, as if leading the way. You take in the beautiful smell of flowers, the songs of birds, and the vividness of everything around you.

Soon you reach your destination. If you are to meet an elf shaman, you will find yourself in an ancient grove of trees. You can find a Celtic shaman in such a grove also. Fairy shamans are usually found at the edge of a forest or near a pool surrounded by flowers. Shamans of other Earth cultures can be discovered in jungles, great plains of grass, or just about anywhere they choose. The same applies to the powerful dragon shamans.

Introduce yourself, and ask for the shaman's name. The shaman may, or may not, give you his or her name upon this first meeting. Ask the shaman if there is anything the shaman needs to tell or show you. Listen closely to what is said, for often references to symbols will be made. These symbols will either have a meaning in your present life or may be clues to remembering past lives.

If you or someone you know has a health problem, ask for a shamanic healing. Unless you are asked to do certain things to help, just sit quietly while the shaman works. When the shaman is finished, he or she may give you some suggestions on what you need to study to improve your spiritual path. Usually, shamans will also take you to meet other shamans or spirits they believe will benefit you. You may even be allowed to sit in on a large shamanic drumming circle or participate in a dance.

When it is time for you to return to your body, the shaman will clap his or her hands loudly. You will find yourself peacefully back in your physical body.

(End of meditation)

Sooner or later, every person who meditates wants to explore different parts of the Otherworld. It is normal to be curious about such a fascinating place, a world that occupies the same time-space as our physical world yet whose higher vibrations make it invisible to our ordinary senses. So I invite you to join me on a scenic tour of the Otherworld, the very real home of spirits, mythological beings, and powerful entities that want very much to help you in any way they can. I will point out ways to discover those helpers already with you, and various methods of attracting others.

It will be helpful if you read the appendix, which explains in more detail about the various areas of the Otherworld. Don't worry about accidentally getting into the Underworld; you simply won't be allowed to go there.

This is a longer meditation, but well worth the time and effort. By doing this meditation, you will be completely familiar with the Otherworld, know where you are when you travel, and can plan ahead exactly what part you want to visit again.

In later chapters, we will explore together the accessible realms of angelic company, and how to work with angels for physical, mental, emotional, and spiritual aid, growth, and development. We will discuss the topics of saints and ascended masters and mistresses. I hope all your journeys, especially the tour of the Otherworld, will be exciting and enlightening for you, journeys that make you open new avenues of thought on your spiritual path.

Exploring the Otherworld Meditation

(Use the cleansing method mentioned on page 16, and the meditation beginning practices listed on page 23.)

As you arrive at the gates to the beautiful Otherworld, you will see your spirit guide who is waiting for you. This guide tells you that you are in the Middleworld, a section much like our earth plane but with more vivid colors and sounds, as well as many different types of creatures. Elves, fairies, dragons, and other mythological creatures are found here, as well as other guides and some animal allies.

As you stroll along a series of paths that lead through beds of flowers and small groves of trees, your guide points out different temples and sacred areas. You may join groups of students listening to a teacher speaking on an interesting subject. Or you may choose to go to one of the temples for a time.

Your guide explains that there are gates in the Middleworld that lead to separate side areas used for specific purposes, as well as some that lead to the Upperworld and Lowerworld. The Upperworld and Lowerworld also have similar gates for travel. All it takes is thinking of a particular place you want to go, and you will be instantly transported there.

One side area is where you find the Seers of All Time and the Web Weavers, among other small, specialized groups. The Seers is an all-female group composed of very ancient, powerful deities from Earth's history, as well as powerful seers from other worlds in the Multiverse. The Web Weavers work with present and potential future events on all worlds.

Another area that might interest you is that of the Akasha Recorders. It is their responsibility to keep the Akashic Records up-to-date for every person and advise the judges who oversee the rebirth process. If you decide to check into your own records, you can visit the Temple of Akashic Records, where assistants are ready to help you find, read, and understand your past lives. This is a good way to determine what part of your past still affects your present life, and could affect your future unless you make changes.

There is no use to visit the Temple of Akashic Records unless you are willing to see the truth and are prepared to learn from past mistakes. To do this, you must discover why you don't care for, or why you have problems with, certain people. Look for repeating negative patterns. It is highly unlikely that you will find you've been a famous person. Ordinary people outnumber the famous, and work harder on balancing karmic residue.

And don't get caught in the web of "looking for your life's purpose." Everyone's goal is the same. Live as good a life as you can, and grow spiritually. Be the best person you can be. You may never know the people you influence for the better by your actions and words.

The area called Four Hidden Dragons is only accessible if you are a serious student of dragon magick. However, you may be granted entrance so that you can go on to an ancient Mystery School where you can learn forgotten techniques. If entrance isn't granted at this time, it simply means you need to do more personal study or that you have chosen the wrong school. Talk to your guide about this, and try again later.

Dragon World is the area for dragon families to raise their young and relax with their families when they aren't working elsewhere.

Faery Land is a side region where you can meet fairies and elves. These beings are not the same, and both species have more than one size of entity. The Fae are human-sized fairies who have a long history of teaching their magick to humans. The Small Folk are the tiny winged fairies who care for plants, flowers, and trees. Just as there are the Seelie (Light) and Unseelie (Dark) Fae, the Light elves and Dark elves are the two clans of their species; they are also human-sized. The name *Dark* doesn't mean "evil." Rather, it describes a difference of energy that is used. It takes a blend of both positive and negative energy to produce magickal changes and results.

The Grove of Shadows and Twilight can be frightening, with its wandering paths that never reach the same place twice. You will find your Shadow Self and any pieces of your shattered soul (a shamanic term) here. Until you have a lot of experience journeying, it would be best if you only entered this grove accompanied by your shaman guide. You won't come to harm if you go in by yourself, but you will find it difficult to understand what you see and what you should do about it.

A compound of many different types of temples, called the Temple of Ancient Ways, has teachers of every religion that did or does exist on earth. These instructors and counselors will talk to you about various spiritual paths, or simply help you learn something new.

The beautiful Gardens of Healing, similar to those in the Upperworld, are the place to learn healing methods, or merely to get a healing yourself.

The Gate of Balance is near the Sacred Well of Balance in the Middleworld. Here, the great greenish-golden dragon Tiamat can help you see through all the illusions that you, or others, have built in your life. Only the truth can be seen if you drink the water of this well or gaze into its depths. Tiamat will answer any questions you might have, so you can better understand any problems.

You can also enter the Lowerworld through this Gate. The vibrations of the Lowerworld seem heavier than those of the Middleworld. Your ancient ancestors can be found here. The Sacred Cauldron of Rebirth lies in a deep, shadowy area of this level. Whenever you go through a traumatic time in your life, or you undergo an initiation, you have the right to step into this cauldron. It will help change the inner pain of trauma, and will change the alignment of your soul's purpose after an initiation.

The Hall of Justice and Rebirth with its powerful Council is also in the Lowerworld. Every soul that chooses reincarnation must come before this Council, where karmic debts are discussed. You may also petition the Council to renegotiate karmic debts that you feel are outdated, no longer practical to spiritual growth, or unattainable in the present situation with certain people.

There is only one level below or joined to the Lowerworld—the Underworld. You will not be allowed to enter that level. This is the place where truly evil souls, not in a reincarnation, are imprisoned.

The Upperworld can be reached easily from the Middleworld. It is a level of very high vibrations and great beauty. All the deities of all ancient religions are found here, as well as the powerful Gardens of Healing. The Gate to the Highest is here, but you can't enter. On the other side of this gate are the Goddess and the God, who are in constant communication with an abstract power we call the Supreme Creative Force, for lack of better words. This

Gate is made of open-work bars, through which you can communicate with the Lord and Lady. Only angels and archangels come and go to the Highest.

A side area of this level contains the Time-Flight and Astra-Keepers. The Dome of Multiversal Stars is kept by the Time-Flight beings; here you can see the exact placement of every star and world in the Multiverse, projected onto the huge black dome. The Astra-Keepers are responsible for creating correct natal charts to match the lives that will be lived by reincarnating souls. They may also discuss your chart with you, if you wish.

The Upperworld is a place of great wisdom. You may meet your guardian angels here, or find very wise elders to teach you something special about yourself and your spiritual path.

When you are finished with your Otherworld explorations, think of your physical body. You will quickly and easily slip back into your body.

(End of meditation)

Helpful Associations

Sometimes, we need a little added help with our spiritual and magickal work. Unless we are very fortunate, nearly all the hours we are awake we are working with our left, or linear, brain. That side is pure practicality (as it views things) and not going to let us start using the more open right brain if it can prevent it. So the trick is to fool the left brain with something that appears to be stable and practical, while the right brain is busy working on magick and with the Otherworld guides, guardians, angels, and other beings.

One method is to set up a small space with a table for magick and/or meditation. You can put anything there that represents your spirit guides, including candles and incense, flowers and stones. By continuing to use the same space for meditation, we trick the left brain into observing the physical objects and considering this a brief rest period, while the right brain kicks in and contacts your spirit friends.

If you want to use holy water to sprinkle about your meditation space, it is possible for you to easily make your own. Add an eighth of a cup of rose water to two quarts of purified water. If you wish, you can also add a quarter of a teaspoon of sea salt. Place both your hands on the bottle of water, and ask firmly that the water be filled with spiritual light and positive vibrations. If you want to add a little more energy to the bottle, let it sit in the light of the full moon for one night. Keep it tightly capped and stored away from sunlight.

Candles and incense are nice additions, but some people can't tolerate any kind of smoke. When using incense, be sure you have very adequate ventilation. With candles, be certain they are in fireproof holders and not near anything that will catch fire. You would be surprised how far heat radiates from a lighted candle. If you don't want to burn a candle, you can have one of an appropriate color sitting on the table.

All guides appreciate your having something on your table to represent them, such as a cultural symbol. Healing teachers and guides will often desire to be represented by green or gold candles. Pink also can be for healing, as well as for spiritual awakening. Blue represents inspiration and opening psychic powers. Brown helps you to communicate with nature spirits, and yellow inspires creativity. However, white works for everything, just as frankincense incense does.

Certain stones are also traditionally associated with spirit guides and teachers. Before you choose a stone, it is wise to read up on it further to see if it can be cleansed with water. Some stones, such as selenite and calcite, will dissolve if placed in liquid of any kind. Some stones are also very fragile and should be kept wrapped, except when in use, to prevent breakage and chipping. Although I don't agree with everything the authors say, I recommend *The Book of Stones* by Robert Simmons and Naisha Ahsian. Cassandra Eason's books are very good, too.

Any piece of quartz crystal can be used for all your guides, teachers, guardians, and angels, plus it aids you in meditations. However, there are certain types of quartz crystal that have more power than others.

An Isis crystal has one facet of the tip that is made up of five sides. A record keeper has raised, indented, or internal triangular designs. Ordinarily the triangles point upward toward the tip. On rare occasions, a crystal will have a triangle pointing downward; these are very good helpers for shamanic soul retrievals. A teacher crystal will have a human-type image inside it, while devic and spirit crystals have images of nature spirits or spirit guides. These images, which may also include fairies, elves, and mythological creatures, are white formations inside the stone. It is not unusual for an image to appear in a stone that had no image before.

Selenite, especially a satin spar wand, is a fascinating stone but can't be cleansed with liquid. It is soft, fragile, and chips easily. However, its smooth, satiny surface gives off gentle vibrations, sometimes even a dreamy mood. The unpolished pieces tend to break off in long shards or crumble. It may take some searching, but you can find selenite in polished wands; spheres; and pointed, cathedral-like formations.

Other stones that help with spirit-guide and teacher communication are pink tourmaline, Apache tear, kyanite, lapis lazuli, kunzite, danburite, ametrine, purple fluorite, azurite, blue chalcedony, amazonite, as well as petrified wood and fossils.

Mythological creatures like chrysoprase, quartz crystal, and pink calcite. Dragons are quite fascinated by rutilated quartz with tiny gold fibers inside.

If you wish to contact certain of your ancient ancestors, perhaps those you meet during your tour of the Otherworld, try selenite, apatite, amber, or petrified wood.

Shaman guides are comfortable with leopardskin jasper (long called the shaman's stone); amber; iolite; purple or black jade; sodalite; spider jasper, with its web-like markings; quartz; and labradorite, with its fish-scale shimmer.

Fairies, elves, devas, and other nature spirits respond best to Apache tears, fairy wand quartz, chlorite (green) phantom quartz, faden veil crystal (which looks like a thin fuzzy white string inside), a naturally bored holey stone, pink calcite, staurolite, moss agate, tree agate, green tourmaline, green fluorite, watermelon (pink and green) tourmaline, phantom crystal, blue chalcedony, moldavite (which is actually the result of an ancient meteor strike), devic crystal, kunzite, amber, and rainforest jasper.

Choose a stone that feels good to you when you hold it in the palm of your hand. If possible, hold it under cool running water before using it. If you're in doubt, gently wipe it with an only-slightly damp cloth and swish it through incense smoke for cleansing. The size of the stone has nothing to do with its power and suitability for what you want to do. In the case of stones, bigger doesn't mean better.

Give the stone and yourself time to become accustomed to each other's vibrations. Place it on your meditation table and handle it often. Hold it while meditating, or at least set it close to you. You can even mount the stone in some type of setting, and wear it.

Enjoy your stone helpers, but try to prevent others from handling them. You want your vibrations on the stones, not someone else's. Stones do attract people, so be prepared to cleanse your stone tools if someone touches them. The best way to avoid this problem is either to keep them covered while on your table or to put them all in a nice box with a lid. Being out of sight prevents some visitor from saying "Oh, look at this!" and starting to grab the stones. Of course, you will have the occasional ill-mannered snoop that even closed boxes don't deter.

Chants, Petitions, and Spells

Meditation is listening for spirit messages of help; prayer, chants, and spells are ways to ask for help. If you don't ask for help with your problems or desires, spirit guides, teachers, and the angels will assume you aren't really all that interested in the outcome. Everyone has free will, so if you want help, you have to ask for it!

Concentrated thought produces energy, which can be formed into matter. Put your energy into a pinpoint of intention and allow it to manifest. Miracles do happen. They do not go against Multiversal laws; the manifestation of miracles is simply accomplished by laws with which we are not yet acquainted.

In the following examples of asking for help, you can use the names Goddess or God, the name of a deity, or whatever title fits into your spiritual path. Each example will be given in Goddess, Pagan, and New Age style, so you have choices.

Guides, teachers, power animals, guardians, and angels are never worshiped. They are honored and respected only as special friends. Worship is reserved for the Goddess, the God, or whatever name you use to designate the abstract power that made everything.

Meet Your Spirit Guide

Goddess Version

Best time: The waxing (getting larger) or full moon. Needs: One white candle, rose incense, and a special small stone or symbol that speaks to you of spiritual guidance. If you plan to carry the stone or symbol in a pouch, you will also need to put this on the altar.

Light the candle and the incense on your altar. Hold the stone or symbol, while you sit or stand before the altar. Repeat the chant three times. Say:

Lady of the earth, the sky, the seas, the moonlit night
Mother of all things that have been, are, and will be
I ask your aid in my quest to meet my true spirit guide.
I ask that this guide will be clearly seen or felt
So no doubts enter my mind about our meeting.
I desire with all my heart for this companionship
This lifelong friend who will remain when all others fade away.
I place this desire within your powerful hands
Knowing that you will answer my petition quickly.

Wave the stone or symbol through the heat above the candle flame, then through the incense smoke. Snuff out

the candle. You can wear or carry this object, or leave it on
the altar.

Pagan Version

*Best time and needs: The same as in the Goddess version, except
substitute a quartz crystal as the stone. You will also need a metal
bowl, a small piece of paper, a pen, and a little holy water. Place
all your items on the altar before casting the circle. You may call
upon your deities by name, or simply call the Lord and Lady.
Cast a circle according to the instructions in the appendix, on page
162.*

Stand before the altar and raise both palms in a salute.

*Lord and Lady, I send this call
Into the Otherworld's highest plane.
I desire with all my heart and soul
To see my guide and hear a name.
I welcome my chosen spirit companion
By powers of Earth, Air, Fire, and Sea.*

(Pick up the crystal in your power hand.)

*This crystal will aid in our connection.
As I do will, so shall it be.*

(Hold the quartz crystal up so it can be seen.)

*By the power of this stone, a cell of Mother Earth
I pledge to open my mind to all true knowledge.*

Lightly sprinkle water on the crystal. Then wave it through
the heat above the candle and through the incense smoke.
If the stone is set in jewelry, put it on now. If not, put it
into a pouch to carry or leave it on your altar.

Sign your name on the small piece of paper and date
it. Say:

Here is my oath, my sacred troth.

Light the paper from the candle and drop it into the metal bowl to burn.

Close the circle according to the directions in the appendix, on page 166. Snuff out the candle.

New Age Version

Put a white or pink rose in a small vase on your altar, along with a candle of the same color. Light the candle and rose incense. Sit comfortably while holding the stone you've chosen to represent your spirit guide. When you are relaxed, look at the stone and say:

Spirit guide, please come to me
And show yourself with clarity.
I need your knowledge to light each day
To keep me on a spiritual way.

Now pray to the Goddess or the God in your own words, asking for help to communicate with your spirit guide.

Sit quietly for a few moments with your eyes closed. Be aware of any feelings of warmth and love, even a small light hug. This will be your guide's way of announcing his or her presence.

Snuff out the candle. Either wear your stone or leave it near the rose on your altar.

Conquering Fear and Negative Thoughts

Goddess Version

Best time and needs: Waning (getting smaller) moon or new moon. A blue candle to represent inner peace and higher vibrations. Frankincense or patchouli incense. A straight sewing pin or needle. The stone that represents your spirit guide. If you wish to have a continuous power supply on your altar, leave a quartz-crystal cluster there. Clusters also cleanse other stones that are left on them overnight.

Carefully push the pin into the candle about one-fourth of an inch from the top. Light the candle and the incense. Say:

All negatives and fear are washed away.
Only true courage with me will stay.
Goddess, your power will help me win
The battle of negative and fear within.
For you gave me free will of my destiny.
Now as I do wish, so shall it be.

Sit quietly with your eyes closed. Mentally visualize each fear and negative habit, one by one. Silently, but with force, tell each to be gone, and see yourself pushing it away. Continue this visualization technique until the candle burns down to the pin. Snuff out the candle.

Whenever you repeat this chant, move the pin down another quarter of an inch before lighting the candle.

Pagan Version

Best time: As given above. Needs: The same as above. This spell can also be used to overcome bad habits.

Carve your name onto the side of the candle with the pin. Put it in the holder and light it.

Stand facing your altar, while raising both hands in salute to your chosen deities. Say:

Lord and Lady, I greet you with joy, and I thank you for joining me in this effort to improve myself. Keep me on my spiritual path so that I may inspire others by my positive actions.

Holding the stone for your spirit guide in one hand, go to the east. Raise your other hand in salute. Say:

Hear me, all spirits and entities of the east and Air.
Cleanse me of all fear and negative habits of the mind.

Go to the south. Raise your hand in salute. Say:

Hear me, all spirits and entities of the south and Fire.
Cleanse me of all fear and negative habits of the spirit.

Go to the west. Raise your hand in salute. Say:

Hear me, all spirits and entities of the west and Water.
Cleanse me of all fear and negative habits of the emotions.

Go to the north. Raise your hand in salute. Say:

Hear me, all spirits and entities of the north and Earth.
Cleanse me of all fear and negative habits of the body.

Return to the altar. Lay your guide stone next to the blue candle. Say:

I ask for guidance from all my spirit guides, teachers, guardians, power animals, and angels. Read my heart, and know that I speak the truth. I release to you all fears, negative thoughts, and harmful habits, so that my life may improve.

Stand quietly for a few moments. Then extinguish the candle and close the circle. Save the blue candle so you can use it again to repeat this ritual as needed.

New Age Version
Best time and needs: Same as above.

Light a blue candle on your altar table. Hold your guide stone while staring at the candle flame for a moment or two. Close your eyes and visualize the bright flame in front of you. See this flame turn to a silvery white as it completely surrounds and fills your body. Feel it transmuting all fear and negative energy into positive energy and joy. Say three times:

Spiritual light destroys all fear.
Nothing negative can exist here.
Be gone, all negatives!

Feel any negative residue draining out of your body and spirit through your feet and into the earth. Say:

Only the Light is seen in me.
By the power of the Highest, I am now free.

Extinguish the blue candle and save it for future workings.

3. GUARDIANS

History of Guardians

No one knows for certain how far back in human history we were aware of the companionship of spirit guides and guardians. Since humans appear to have always had some type of spiritual belief, I suspect we knew about these Otherworld companions from the beginning. These invisible beings are found in every culture's history. The names for them are not all the same, but the descriptions of their abilities and activities certainly are.

Fortunately, I love this kind of research. Put me in a room full of history and mythology books, hand me the end of a fragile thread on a vague spiritual idea, and my interest is immediately engaged. How far back does this idea go? Is it found in just certain cultures, or does it leap cultural boundaries to touch all? Has the idea remained consistent or has it changed through the centuries? Where did it change, and why? What is the basic truth behind it all?

If I discover some buried, ancient truth that can be of use today, I try to write about it in such a manner that it is of practical use to other seekers. Often, I uncover ancient truths and wisdom that have no practical application yet in daily living or magick. I file my notes about these interesting discoveries with the hope that someday someone will see their use and present them to readers.

The subject of personal and clan guardians resonates throughout all cultures. Usually, the guardians were looked upon as powerful friends. In a few cultures, however, they were viewed as unstable in nature and had to be propitiated in some manner to keep on their good side. In the shamanistic cultures, it was not uncommon for it to be taboo to eat the flesh of your personal power animal.

When one mentions guardians, most people immediately think of guardian angels. Terms equivalent to *guardian angel* appeared first in Persia, India, and ancient Sumeria. Since the word *angel* is actually of Greek origin, a variety of other terms were used to identify these Otherworld beings who have such high vibrations. However, since the word *angel* is widely understood, I will use that word for these beings, regardless of the culture explored.

However, there are far more available guardians than most of us realize. Huge numbers of these Otherworld beings are simply waiting to be acknowledged so that they can work more closely with humans. The old saying goes that to attract friends you should be friendly. So open your mind, expect surprises, and go searching for as many guardians as you would like.

Never assume that you can't meet these beings. Never let anyone convince you that your goals are impossible. Believe in yourself. Miracles are universal laws in action, laws we haven't learned about yet.

Everyone has psychic senses, paranormal senses, or para-senses. You just have to exercise them as you would a physical muscle so that they work better. Keep trying. They will usually begin to work when you least expect it.

Types of Guardians and Meditations

Guardians come in all shapes, sizes, nationalities, and types of beings. Every human has at least two, if not more. However, most people think of them only in terms of guardian angels because of the Middle Eastern and European cultural influences. A great number of people are not aware of the many types of beings who qualify for, and frequently fill, the position of guardian. With just a little more information and awareness, you can fill in the knowledge gaps and expand your spiritual friendships.

Guardians frequently first appear in the unobtrusive forms called intuition and premonitions. I've heard this explained as rousing the sleeping sentry of the subconscious mind, which is as good an explanation as any. Always take note of these circumstances, as they are both warnings and evidence of your guardian spirits.

Each of us attracts a number of spirit companions and guardians as we go through life. Some of these will be deceased loved ones, who may frequently check on your progress and well-being. Since most souls put at least a hundred years or more between incarnations, many of your distant ancestors could pay you a visit at any time. Old friends from past lives also take the opportunity to stop by from time to time to renew acquaintances, at least on a subconscious level.

My father, who died before he was fifty, has proved to be a guardian on more than one occasion. I suddenly woke one night to the sound of my deceased father calling my name. I looked through my open bedroom door to see the living room full of waist-high smoke. Naturally, I jumped up to investigate and discovered that the "smoke" was psychic mist. I wandered through the house, lit only by moonlight, and felt I should check the furnace motor. It felt hot to the touch but there was no burning odor. I tried to get my then-husband to have it checked, but he was going out of town the next day and wouldn't. Two days later, just as I prepared for bed, I heard my father call again. This time I could smell hot smoke. I immediately turned off the furnace and found that the motor had begun to smoke. It had to be replaced.

On some occasions, certain human guardians, in spirit form, may suddenly appear to help you because of the situation or events in which you are embroiled. These guardians have fought for or against similar causes in their past lives and feel a duty to help you in order to serve spiritual justice.

Spirits who choose to accompany you can also be deceased pets. It isn't at all unusual to see a pet lover with several pet spirits close by as companion-guardians. Since there are no boundaries to the animals that people acquire as pets, there are no boundaries as to what these animals may be. The ones that really startle me, though, are snakes, particularly boas. I simply can't feel any friendship with snakes and spiders. Obviously, the person they accompany does though.

Some visitors to our house ask about the small brown-and-white terrier who flits in and out of their vision, along with a number of spirit cats. MacDougal has made it quite clear that he isn't open to another dog being here, although the cats don't seem to mind my bringing in new cats. The invisible cats that rub against visitors' legs seem to upset a number of my visitors. These animals, still very dear to me, are frequently so clear that I step over them as I do the cats that live here now.

Sometimes the accompanying animal spirits are not of earthly incarnation. They belong to what the Celts called *animal allies* and other shamanic societies called *power animals*.

Depending upon your disposition, openness, and attitude, you may find yourself blessed by the company of one or more elemental beings, fairies, elves, or beautiful mythological creatures, such as dragons and unicorns. In fact, if you are friendly and welcoming to these unique beings, you will soon find you have a constant crowd of them. They are fantastic for raising vibrations within your environment. They also are a wellspring of Multiversal energy and information. And the mythical creatures, especially dragons, are powerful protectors.

You may find that at critical moments you feel the presence of a powerful animal (mythical or otherwise). They will infuse your aura and mind with whatever qualities you need to protect yourself, as well as projecting their personal defensive feeling directly at whatever or whoever is making you feel threatened.

Any of the following list of power animals may appear to you in meditation as a symbol of what you need to do or the energies you might need in your aura and life. Or you may see them physically or with your para-senses. If you need to call upon one, assume their mental characteristics into your body as a means of empowering your defense, whether it be physical or verbal against harassment.

Power Animals

Badger: Tenacity in self-defense

Bear: Stamina, balance and harmony, defense, transformation

Butterfly: New life cycle, love, joy

Cat, domestic: Know when to fight, when to retreat. Self-assured. Search for hidden information.

Cobra: Move silently and swiftly in defense. Adapt to necessary life events.

Coyote: Move silently, seize opportunities, illusion

Crow: Prophecy, cunning, skill, knowledge. Secret wisdom to connect with ancient Mysteries and certain deities.

Deer: Swiftness, abundance, guide to spiritual knowledge

Dog: Remove confusion and illusions

Dolphin: Joy in life; wisdom; ancient secrets of Atlantis, Lemuria, and other lost civilizations

Dragon: Protection, transformation, spiritual wisdom, arrival of special teachers

Dragonfly: Dreams, mystical messages, coming changes

Eagle: See behind the human masks everyone wears. Wisdom, swiftness, courage.

Elephant: Remove obstacles, learn new skills, patience

Falcon: Soul-healing, magick, astral travel

Fox: Slyness, wisdom, invisibility. Escape aggressors. Ability to adapt to unusual circumstances.

Frog: New life cycle. Spiritual initiations.

Goose: New beginnings, inspiration

Hawk: Recall past lives, decisiveness, boldness, wisdom

Horse: Endurance, freedom, Otherworld travel guide, overcome obstacles.

Hummingbird: Happiness, relaxation, everyday wisdom

Jaguar: Healing, hidden knowledge, changing future events

Leopard: Cunning, stealth, boldness, confidence

Lion: Strength, courage, release stress

Lizard: Dreams, illusions. Face your fears.

Mouse: Cunning, invisibility, secrets, stealth. Beware of double-talk.

Otter: Wisdom, uncover talents, recover from a crisis

Owl: Silent movement, unmasking deceivers, finding hidden truths

Panther, black: Fierce in defense, move silently, constant awareness for danger

Pegasus: Appearance in a meditation indicates a transforming Otherworld journey. Poetic inspiration.

Phoenix: Renewal, transformation. A troubled time with a positive ending.

Porcupine: Defense when threatened. Break anyone's control over you.

Rattlesnake, rainbow-colored: A powerful symbol of great magickal power and the key to the doors of many Mysteries

Raven: Transformation, messages from spirit, warnings. A symbol of finding treasures in unexpected places.

Scorpion: Return negative energy to the sender. Swiftness in defense. Unforeseen changes.

Snakes, in general: Wisdom, transformation for the better, shedding negatives and old habits

Spiders: Creativity, divine inspiration. As is the case with scorpions, snakes, and some of the other unpredictable power animals, don't call up spider energy without linking it to a more predictable animal.

Squirrel: Changes, balance, raising the level of consciousness

Swallow: Good luck, success

Tiger: Powerful energy to face unpleasant events and fearlessly take action

Turtle and tortoise: Patience, development of new ideas

Unicorn: Prosperity, strength of mind, personal power

Whale: Very ancient magick of lost civilizations. Commune with nature spirits through music.

Winged bull: Supernatural strength, protection, guidance

Wolf: Intelligence, escape aggressors, outwit enemies. Dreams, magick, intuition, protection.

It also isn't unusual for ancient warriors (male or female) or powerful magicians to come to your aid, although their presence may not be constant or consistent. However, all guardians will be at your side immediately when you call upon them, even in thoughts.

Human-sized Fae and elf warriors and magicians can also become human guardians, particularly when you are out in nature. The Fae and elf mystics work on very high spiritual levels, very close to where you will find angels.

Some guardians are never seen, but send strong intuitive signals to make you cautious and more alert to life and to upcoming, difficult events.

The most difficult, and fortunately the least seen, guardian is the Trickster. These guardians force you to learn lessons you are avoiding. They get you into difficult situations so that you will learn to use common sense and strategy to get out—and also so that you won't get into that place again. Tricksters may overdo the teaching at times. If that happens, you need to talk to your spirit guides about the problem.

Nearly everyone has heard stories of guardian angels. We usually assume there is one angel per person. However, in ancient Middle Eastern records we find that guardian angels are mentioned as a pair per person. This idea is still held today in that area. One guardian angel is for guidance and carrying messages to and from the Goddess and the God. The other angel is the recording angel, who writes down our deeds and thoughts in the book of our personal life. Both angels also protect and can ask for leniency and understanding on karmic issues.

The importance and status of either spirit guides or guardians cannot be judged by where you meet them in your Otherworld meditations. Although each person is born with a spirit guide, guardian angels, and a primary guardian, we are so used to their vibrations that it can be difficult to recognize them at first. However, once you make contact with your main personal guardian and become comfortable with this guardian, other guardians, guides, and teachers will appear in order to help you expand your spiritual growth and aid you in certain studies.

Meeting Your Guardian Meditation

(Use the cleansing method mentioned on page 16, and the meditation beginning practices listed on page 23.)

You are standing in a meadow. A path leads through the lush grass to an open gate in a high wall. This wall extends as far as you can see in both directions. You quickly go down the path and through the gate into a beautiful garden. Through the trees you can see temples, groves of other trees, and the shimmering colors of beds of flowers. There are a number of paths, all leading in different directions. You choose one and follow it as it winds alongside a little stream and then over an arched bridge toward several different temples.

You choose a temple that appeals to you in shape and color. As you enter it, a human figure steps forward to meet you. Determine if this being is male or female, and carefully observe the hair, eye, and skin color. This human-formed being is one of your spirit guardians.

Your guardian walks with you around the inside of the temple as the two of you become acquainted. You may get a name or part of a name during this walk. You can ask if the two of you have been together in other lives. If so, your guardian will tell you about that connection.

If your guardian is one of the human-sized Fae (fairy) or an elf, he or she may decide to take you outside for a walk through a sacred grove. Since this area is the Middleworld, your guardian will take you to the Akashic Library if you wish. If your guardian refuses to do so at this time, it is because of the desire to spend more time talking to you about your present life before the two of you explore past lives.

Your guardian may also introduce you to certain teachers who will be working with you on special subjects at a later time. It is possible that other guardians may appear to talk to you. Spend as much time as you wish talking to your guardian and those you meet. You may also be taken to other temples, or you may listen to teachers with groups of students throughout the temple grounds.

When you are finished, your guardian will take you to a brightly lighted gate. As you step into the light, you are quickly and comfortably returned to your physical body.

(End of meditation)

Meeting Power Animals Meditation
(Use the cleansing method mentioned on page 16, and the meditation beginning practices listed on page 23.)

As you relax, you find yourself drifting down a quiet stream in a small boat. You see fish in the water, hear frogs along the banks among the cattails, and watch animals come to the stream to drink. Soon the boat floats through a short tunnel in a huge rock and emerges into a special place. Here, animals, birds, reptiles, and even plants can communicate with you. This is the area where you will meet the power animals that are closest to you at this time. Each time you take this meditation journey, you can renew your bond with your power animals and perhaps meet new ones.

The boat drifts up onto a sandy shore so you can get out and explore. You can wander along the stream, climb the nearby rocks, or venture into the forest. Your power animal or animals will make themselves known to you by appearing three different times. If you are uncomfortable with any that appear, politely thank them—but tell them you don't feel ready yet to work with their energies. If they persist in appearing, it means that you definitely do need to learn to handle their energies. There may be a future event in motion that will require you to use the energy of that particular power creature.

Since all beings here can communicate easily, you can talk to them about what is happening in your life and how to handle it. Or they can show you how to mentally "put on" their characteristics when needed.

If you wish, you can meld your astral body with theirs, and see the life around you from their viewpoint. This practice also helps you to better understand how to feel and use their energy. Spend as much time with your power animals as you wish.

When you are ready to return to your physical body, go back to the stream and sit in the boat. It will float back into the tunnel of rock. As you enter the tunnel, you will feel yourself sliding back into your physical body.

(End of meditation)

Meeting Your Guardian Angels Meditation

Angels can be very helpful in helping to renegotiate karmic links that are no longer appropriate or necessary. I have noticed over the years that, even when karmic lessons are learned and debts are paid, we frequently hold onto the karmic pattern out of habit. This is very true if the lesson or debts have continued through several lifetimes and with the same people involved. It is difficult for each of us to impartially look at our own karmic patterns and know if we have finished them or not. However, your guardian angels do know the truth. If we haven't quite gotten all the lessons, they can also ask that the intensity of the karmic lesson be eased so this life is more comfortable.

(Use the cleansing method mentioned on page 16, and the meditation beginning practices listed on page 23.)

See yourself standing at the foot of a stairway that leads up from the Middleworld into the clouds. As you quickly move up the stairs and pass through the snowy banks of mist, you find yourself near the golden gate to the highest Otherworld realm. Through the bars of the gate you can see the Goddess and the God sitting close together. You realize that their duality is the manifestation of the Supreme Creative Form that no being, except angels, ever sees, hears, or understands.

If you wish, you may speak to the Goddess and the God through the gate. Or you can visit any of the magnificent gardens and temples you see around you. As you walk, you see two brightly glowing figures coming toward you. They are human in appearance, except for their aura energy that flows from between their shoulder blades in what looks like great feathery wings. These are your two guardian angels. They may or may not give you their names at this time. Remember, although angels look like humans, they are far more detached emotionally than we are. However, your guardian angels can be much more sympathetic, loving, and understanding of your problems than other angels are. They are with you when you are born into this life, and remain with you through death of the body. Along with your spirit guides, personal guardian angels advocate for you before the Council about karmic debts.

Your angels greet you with love and compassion. They are happy that you have chosen to recognize their existence and help. They lead you to a small, quiet temple, where you can talk with them about any part of your life. You may have questions about upcoming decisions, or you may ask them for help in renegotiating karmic problems with people or events. If certain karmic relationships, for example, keep coming into your life, your angels can tell you why and suggest what you could do to halt this. If you have habits or addictions that you want to release, they can point out ways to release these.

Many times we erroneously think that diseases are karmic, when they actually are not. If you have a disease or disability, you may have chosen it to learn compassion or to teach compassion to others. Your angels will help you understand the reasons behind such events. They can also heal your body, mind, emotions, and spirit. If the bodily disease is not to be healed, they will give you the strength and understanding to work through it. They will help you find ways to use your trouble for good.

You may ask your angels any questions you wish. You may also ask them to show you around the Upperworld, for there are many exquisite temples, libraries, and special gardens there. They can even help you find deceased loved ones whom you may wish to see again.

When you are ready to leave, your guardian angels take you back to the shining stairway leading down through the clouds. As you walk down the stairway, you find yourself slipping comfortably into your physical body.

(End of meditation)

Helpful Associations

If you use colored candles for meditations or spells, you will find that nature spirits and power animals respond best to pink, green, and brown. Spirit guides and teachers are attracted to blues, while guardians often like purple. Guardian angels like gold or silver. However, the color white will work for any of these beings.

Stones seem to be of interest to all beings, whether human or from the Otherworld. Many stones are traditionally connected with certain beings. Stones connected to guardians are cat's-eye, fire agate, amazonite, ametrine, blue chalcedony, garnet, hematite, lepidolite, mahogany obsidian, malachite, red jasper, smoky quartz, and tourmaline.

Power animals have been connected with certain powerful shamanic stones throughout human history, including rutilated quartz (dragons), snow quartz (unicorns), and leopardskin jasper and tiger-eye (the cat family). Jet, amber, and obsidian work for nearly any power animal, as does crystal quartz.

Angelite, apophyllite, crystal quartz, amethyst, and selenite are helpful during meditations and prayers to contact and communicate with your guardian angels.

Remember, the size of the stone has little to do with its power available to you. The smallest piece of quartz crystal can be an enormous amplifier when focused upon properly.

There is one other type of guardian that people frequently overlook—an invisible energy guardian created for the specific purpose of protecting a house, property, pets, and/or a vehicle. Although you can create this energy guardian and simply set it on a shelf or table, it is much easier to remember where you actually placed it if you anchor it to a statue. Dragons and gargoyles are particularly good anchors, and seem to hold the energy longer than simply using a blank space.

If you plan to use a statue as an anchor, set the statue so that it faces the primary doorway into your home. This statue doesn't have to be large or ornate, nor does it have to be at eye level. To create this very personal guardian, rub the palms of your hands together. Slowly move your hands apart until the tingling energy between them begins to feel weaker. As you are collecting and compacting psychic energy, verbally or mentally tell the energy what you want it to do as your guardian. Direct it to protect your house, property, family, and pets. Tell this guardian that it is welcome to eat all the negative energy that enters your personal area.

At this point, form the invisible energy into a ball with your hands, smoothing the outer layer into a shell. You will be able to feel the ball between your hands, even though your physical eyes will probably not register its existence. Lower your hands over the statue, like slipping a cover over it. The tingling energy will transfer from your hands into its new home.

At least once a week, rub your palms together and add more energy to the guardian. You will be able to feel the protective power grow as the tingling ball gets bigger. Also, thank your special guardian on a regular basis.

You can also create a similar guardian for each vehicle, if you wish. Instead of a statue to anchor the energy ball, simply attach it to the rearview mirror. The same procedure can be used on motorcycles and bicycles, or any kind of child vehicle or transportation toy that a child might ride.

I've seen some amazing reactions by people who are not aware of these invisible guardians. The most common phenomena seem to be either they don't notice the statue at all, even though it is in plain view, or those people who always want to touch everything will get shocked by static electricity.

If you want to create a guardian for loved ones who live elsewhere, you can attach the energy ball to a photo of that person or people.

Chants, Petitions, and Spells

Chants, spells, and prayers are asking the Higher Force for something you desire. Meditation is listening for answers.

Magickal spells, even forceful prayers that are spells, are the focusing of your power on a desired outcome. That focus must be like a laser beam, so real to you that you don't doubt its existence or right to manifest.

The trick, for lack of a better word, is to want and work for the result you desire with all your heart and emotions, but then let go of those strong emotions as you release the magickal energy at the end of a spell. If you keep thinking and talking about your desire, you pull that energy back toward you and weaken it so that nothing happens.

It is wise to use the cleansing method mentioned on page 16, especially when you work on protection and banishing spells. The cleaner your auras and chakras are, the less likely any negative energy will stick to you. In both banishing and protection spells, you are using Otherworld energy to amplify your own power so that you can either return the negative energy to the sender or ground it into the earth. A return-burn is often the only way to teach a troublemaker to stop sending negative magick, especially if the person or group in question insists on repeating the offense.

Overcome a Bad Habit

Goddess Version

Best time: Waxing or full moon, or on a Friday. Needs: A black candle to represent the bad habits and a white candle to represent you in your healed state. A small nail.

If possible, do this ritual three times, beginning two days before the full moon and ending on the full-moon night itself.

Using the nail, scratch the name of the bad habit on the black candle. Place it in a fireproof holder on the left side of your altar. Scratch your name on the white candle. Put it in a holder on the right side of your altar.

Light the black candle, and make a pushing-away motion with your left hand. Light the white candle, and wave your hand toward your heart. Say:

> *Goddess of the sky, the earth, the sea*
> *Grant me this boon I ask of thee.*
> *I walk away from harmful things.*
> *I walk into the Light.*
> *I draw my strength from endless Love*
> *And from this win my fight.*

Let the candles burn out. Dispose of the wax in the garbage—a fitting place for bad habits or addictions.

Accept a Situation

Pagan Version

Best time: Anytime. Needs: Candles set at the four directions: east, yellow; south, red; west, blue; north, dark green.

Be sure the candles are each in a fireproof holder and set in a place where they will not set anything on fire.

Since this spell is an acceptance of a difficult life event, you may want to do this spell followed by a meditation with your guardian angels. At the end of the meditation, you may extinguish the candles and use them again for the same work.

Light the yellow candle in the east, and say:

All beings of the east and the element of Air, be with me during this time of trouble.

Light the red candle, and say:

All beings of the south and the element of Fire, be with me during this time of trouble.

Light the blue candle. Say:

All beings of the west and the element of Water, be with me during this time of trouble.

Light the dark green candle. Say:

All beings of the north and the element of Earth, be with me during this time of trouble.

Sit in preparation for your meditation with your guardian angels. Before you begin the meditation, say:

I accept my karma to be in this time and place.

Give me the strength and courage to endure what I must.

Grant me the peace and wisdom I need to endure.

After your meditation, extinguish the candles—beginning in the east and ending in the north.

Heal a Negative Situation

New Age Version
Best time: Waning or new moon. Needs: A small piece of paper on which you have written out the situation, a metal bowl to burn the paper in, and a white candle.

Set the white candle in the center of your altar. Light it and ask for healing energy to surround you. Place the metal bowl and the paper in front of the candle.

Read the paper aloud and make any changes you think are necessary. Fold the paper in half, and then in half again. Light it with the white candle and drop the paper into the bowl to burn, while saying:

All that was broken is mended.
All that was wrong is made right.
All darkness and hurt are banished.
All that remains is the Light.

Sit for a few moments while you project pure white light toward the negative situation and any people involved. This spell can be repeated as often as necessary.

Banishing

Pagan or New Age Version
(Best time: Waning or new moon; however, use whenever necessary. Needs: A mirror that can easily be held in your hand, preferably with one magnifying side.)

With this spell, you don't have to know the responsible ill-wisher or spell-sender. You just need to realize that you've had a run of sudden bad luck, all the way from dented fenders down to unusual clumsiness, unexpected drains on your finances, or bad health.

Stand quietly and call upon your personal guardian, or ask for a guardian warrior to help you with this spell.

Begin by facing east, holding the magnifying mirror facing away from you. Visualize your guardian spirit's image projecting out of the mirror. Say:

In a mirror, bright, not dark, an awesome figure reflects its form.

Into a barrier, protective, fierce. I stand behind it safe from harm.

No threats can reach me, here behind. No magick reaches to my heart.

The mirror sends evil back to source. O evil powers, now depart!

Turning clockwise, face each direction and repeat the spell. After chanting to the north, turn back to face the east, thus sealing you inside a protective bubble.

Bind a Harmful Person or Enemy

Pagan Version
(Best time: Waning or new moon. Needs: A small and ordinary rock, patchouli oil, and a dark purple candle.)

Light the purple candle and place it in the center of your altar. Anoint the rock with patchouli oil. Wave it in the heat above the candle. While visualizing the harmful person, hold the rock and project the person's image into it. Say:

One to seek her/him. One to find her/him.
One to bring her/him. One to bind her/him.
To this stone, forever one.
So say I. This spell is done.

Wrap the rock in a tissue until you can either throw it into running water or in an isolated place in nature.

Stop Harmful Gossip

Goddess, Pagan, or New Age Version
(Best time: Waning or new moon. Needs: A dark purple candle for justice, a metal bowl, a paper on which you draw a rough human outline and write the names of the gossips.)

Be certain you are not simply looking for revenge on people repeating facts. If you are, you will feel repercussions from this spell.

Light the purple justice candle in the center of your altar. Draw the rough human outline complete with eyes and mouth. Place the metal bowl beside the candle with the paper spread flat nearby.

Take the candle and carefully drop one drop of wax on the drawing's mouth. Say:

Your mouth is stopped.

Place one drop of wax on each eye, and say:

Your eyes see naught.

Put a drop of wax on the center of the head. Set the candle back in its holder. Say:

Your thoughts are bound.
Your words turn 'round.
No longer will you bother me.
This is my will. So shall it be.

Fold the paper in half. Light it in the candle's flame. Drop it in the bowl to burn as you say:

I call Earth to bind my spell
Air to speed its travel well.

Bright as Fire shall it glow.
Deep as tide of Water flow.
Count the elements fourfold,
And in the fifth, the spell shall hold.

Let the candle burn out. Dispose of the wax and ashes in the garbage.

Obtain Spiritual Blessings

Goddess, Pagan, or New Age Version
(Best time: Waxing or full moon. Needs: A white candle and a piece of jewelry symbolic of your beliefs, or one with a stone that has meaning for you. Holy water is optional.)

This blessing-spell is especially powerful when followed by a meditation to talk with your guides, guardians, teachers, or guardian angels.

Light the white candle. Put it in a fireproof holder in a safe place to burn during your meditation.

If you use holy water, sprinkle a few drops on the jewelry. Wave the jewelry through the heat above the lighted candle. Hold it in your hand while you say:

Blessings I seek to better my life
To chase away darkness, diminish the strife.
To heal me in body, my mind, and my soul
This I request. This is my goal.

Put on the piece of jewelry and wear it while you meditate. At the end of the meditation, extinguish the candle.

4. Relationships of Angels

History of Angels

A great many cultures around the world have believed in beings that we now call angels. These great helpers of humankind are described in nearly all the sacred books of the world religions. Among the ancient cultures and religions that believed in angels are the Egyptians, Romans, Greeks, Persians, Muslims, Japanese Shintoists, Jewish Qabalists, Hindus, and the Maoris.

Some of the world's greatest thinkers and writers also believed in angelic existence. References to angels can be found in the works of Socrates, Plato, Saint Augustine, Paracelsus,

Thomas Moore, William Blake, Shakespeare, Milton, Pythagoras, Homer, Saint Thomas Aquinas, Jacob Boehme, and Emanuel Swedenborg.

The Jewish mystics called angels the "shining ones." The Old and New Testaments, the apocryphal books of the Jews and Christians, and the Koran of Muslims are all full of references to these nonhuman beings, particularly the four main archangels.

The idea behind the Hebrew word *malakh* (angel) comes from the Sanskrit word *angiras*, a divine spirit; from the Persian *angaros*, a courier; and from the Greek *angelos*, a messenger or one sent. The meaning is actually closer to the Greek word *daimon*, a supernatural being who mediates between the Supreme Power and humans. The Hebrews got their basic ideas of angels from their captivity in Persia and Babylon.

The words *devil* and *divinity* both come from the Indo-European words *devi* (Goddess) and *deva* (God); this became *daeva* (devil) in Persian. The devas were either positive or negative, depending upon the event and the need. To explain the change from both Goddess and God, who judged each action as needed, to one male God, the fallen angels and their "leader" were created. Nonbelievers who didn't follow this new one-god religion and obey the church-made laws, and those who still don't, are said to be facing eternal torture. Even the hells mentioned in other religions never keep souls forever to torture. When the soul learns its lesson, it is released to reincarnate.

Archangel is a term applied to the pure spiritual-energy beings who are the leaders of all the ranks (I prefer the word *degrees*) of angels. In both Jewish and Christian literature, archangels are listed as messengers of God, supreme beings, defenders, teachers, and on occasion, punishers. Among the accepted archangels are Michael, Gabriel, Raphael, Uriel (sometimes called Auriel), Raguel, Sandalphon, Haniel, Metatron, Barakiel, Jehudiel, Barbiel, Oriphiel, and Tzadkiel. Even the Koran recognizes the four main archangels under similar names: Mikhail, Jibril, Azrael, and Israfil. Often the names and/or their spelling change from source to source.

Angels are a special species of beings, whose vibrations are so very high and pure that they have access to the Supreme Being. They have never been, and never will be, human as we understand the term *human*, although they have the ability to appear in human form. If seen in a humanlike form, they may look male or female, but most angels do not seem to actually have a gender. We know very little about whether angels reproduce; however, the Book of Enoch says that certain angels called the Watchers did produce children with human women.

The true purpose of angels in both the astral and earthly planes is rather nebulous. No one has a definite answer. They appear on their own schedules and for unknown purposes. Even if an angel works closely with a human, the angel keeps its distance except during the working time. They have been known to create miracles with ease. However, for all their help to humans, we are not to worship them and cannot command them to do anything. They are invincible to all spells. The most a magician can do is sincerely ask for their help.

The Christians firmly believed in angels (which they commonly called *God's messengers*), until the First Council of Nicaea in 352 eliminated much of the writing about angels. Apparently, the early power-holders of this sect were afraid that belief in the help and support of angels would lessen their followers' devotion to Jesus. However, in 1215, at the Lateran Council, the church returned to much of the recognition of the existence of angels. Only this time they heavily preached about Satan (not a personal name as I will explain later) and the evil of the "fallen angels."

Unfortunately, the translators of the sacred books used by the Bible and connected reference books changed the meaning of entire sections of text to better serve whatever they had in mind. Century after century, each new translator made changes until much of the original meaning was lost. The complete true story of the angels became hidden under a pile of personalized opinions until people no longer knew what to believe.

This distortion of angels even seeped over into the medieval paintings, where the mighty cherubim were shown as cupids, fat little *putti* who seemed to like to hang around half-nude women. Perhaps this style of portrayal came about because of the church divisions and arguments over angels during that time. Everyone, including the church, seemed to ignore this distorted artistry; one reason could be because the *putti* looked so innocent and not as threatening as the real cherubim. The actual degree of angels called the cherubim are enormous in size and extremely powerful. If one were to appear in the sky, your mind would not recognize it, for it would fill the entire heavens and beyond.

This situation continued until such noted translators as Professor Elaine Pagels and others gained access to the original Dead Sea Scrolls, the Nag Hammadi Library, scrolls of the Essenes, the Torah, the Bible, and the Gnostic texts. When these new, nonbiased, respected members of universities finished their translations, angels in particular were portrayed in a completely new light. Professor Pagels' work was published in the mid-1990s with little notice or fanfare, as were those of other workers.

I had been uncomfortable with the usual portrait of angels since a child. I was always in trouble with priests and ministers for asking questions. How could they say some angels were all good, yet they destroyed entire cities and armies simply because the people didn't believe in a certain religion? Why was Lucifer considered evil and "thrown out of heaven" because he refused to bow in worship to Adam? Didn't the rest of their Bible say you were to bow to no one but God? Something was wrong with that picture.

As I grew older and became fascinated with mythology and history, I discovered a great many clues that added to my skepticism. For example, until Zoroaster of Persia came up with his idea and religion that "God" and an evil competitor were equally powerful rivals with their bands of angelic followers, no culture or history listed this duality of angels. Nor is there any mention of any other being holding equal power with the esoteric Supreme Creative Power. There had to be a reason that this strange duality appeared, and continued to thrive, in the Middle Eastern area that birthed the religions of the Jews, Christians, and Muslims.

When I finally discovered Professor Pagels' books, everything began to make sense. Zoroaster was simply creating a different religion of which he was the ruler. The Jewish people came in contact with this idea when they were prisoners in Babylon. And being an intelligent culture, when they wrote about their culture's experiences with their adversaries, they used code names to identify enemies. Therefore, the written religious texts of today, riddled with false translations anyway, missed this valuable clue of code names, considering them as something different than was meant in the beginning.

Many of the Jewish adversaries' names were worked into the written texts as followers of Satan. Thus, any outsider who read these texts would not understand and wouldn't be taking revenge for being ridiculed. This has been the historians' way of recording for centuries in that region. Until Pagels and other professors went back to the original texts and retranslated, we didn't have a clue about the truth, starting with the supposed name *Satan*.

Satan was never a personal name of anybody, human or otherwise. The Jewish phrase *ha satan* means "an adversary." This could be applied to every enemy or person who is threatening in any manner, including your grumpy, beer-bellied neighbor who leaves trash in your driveway.

As Dan Brown alludes to in his books *Angels & Demons* and *The Da Vinci Code*, angels as a species are not all to be judged by our definition of wonderful, helping beings. Nor are the so-called "fallen angels" to be considered evil. They also are not demons, which is an entirely different category of negative beings.

Instead of calling this second group of angels "fallen," I prefer the name *Shadow*. They are the energy balance of the Light angels. Anyone in magick knows that both negative and positive energies are needed to manifest anything. Negative doesn't mean "bad" or "evil" either. After all, the leader of the Shadow angels is Lucifer, whose name means "light-bringer." His equal among the Light angels is Michael, who carries a powerful sword and is known as a warrior: a balance of opposites.

Shadow angels were not named as evil until Zoroaster invented his religion. However, there are clues and indirect references to knowledge of their prior existence. They were considered important and within the laws of creation. Later religions simply misinterpreted their character and work. Every ancient culture before Zoroaster that knew about angels didn't classify these Otherworldly beings as being all good or all bad. They were acknowledged as simply existing as very special divine messengers and helpers, as intermediaries between the Supreme Power and humans.

So I decided to share what I've learned about all the angels, both Light and Shadow. What I present certainly won't be all there is to learn, as much of this subject matter is just now being examined.

All angels can appear in many guises and forms, some of which appear human. They can change their appearance according to need. In their true forms, angels are brilliant light shapes, but they can alter to assume racial colors and features to accommodate human expectations.

Some angels are definitely more feminine than masculine in appearance, while others remain androgynous in appearance and actions. They are all brilliantly colored in some manner. These colors can fluctuate or change if they wish, just as their images can.

Some seem to have halos and wings, while others don't. Their wings are really streams of moving energy that propel them from place to place. If your mental, stereotyped image doesn't demand wings, you are unlikely to see wings. Angels try to be accommodating. They certainly don't have to be visible, to you or anyone else, in order to aid humans. Their specialty is what humans call "miracles." Miracles are all around us. We miss them because we aren't paying attention.

How the Two Angelic Realms Work Together

The Multiverse runs on the balancing of negative and positive energy flows for continual manifestation. This includes absorbing whatever matter is disintegrating and reforming it into a new version of itself, or into something altogether different. The same applies to any type of magick; and prayer is magick, too.

Both Light and Shadow angels have distinct, definite roles to play in the proper balance of the Multiverse. Since they are the most closely connected to the Supreme Power, they are a vital link to the existence of everything.

The realms of the angels lie above the area of the Otherworld that is called the Highest. Although the Otherworld isn't really formed of circles, areas, columns, or even layers, diagrams showing it in this manner help us to understand it better. See the Otherworld diagram in the appendix.

Instead of using the orthodox words *choirs* or *ranks* to describe the nine worlds of angels, I will use *degrees*—because it is by degrees that one has any chance of working with most of the angels. And regardless of how intelligent or diligent you are, you will not be able to work to the top tiers of angels. Their vibrations are so much higher than ours that there is no way we can grasp what they really are and what they do. We can only guess that the top angelic tiers work with pure, raw creative power straight from the Supreme Power itself.

In fact, in order to interact with the Multiverse and all creations, the Supreme Power (which has no duality) must step Its vibrations down to a point where duality (positive and negative) is formed. For, without duality, there can be no manifestation of anything. This duality is first manifested in angelic beings, who step the vibrations down even more to produce what we understand are the gods and goddesses, who lower the vibrations still more to produce humans and all other beings and creations.

The subject of the Supreme Power must rest at this point in the discussion, because there is no way we can possibly understand anything that exists or happens above angels. And actually we know very little about *them*. After all the centuries of learning, we are only a few steps up the ladder of knowledge on this subject.

Knowing what we do about the necessity of using opposing types of energy to create, we can readily understand why there are both Light and Shadow angels. We can also recognize why working with both types will produce results, where working with only one type will not.

Please remember that Shadow angels are not evil or demons. Water is necessary for life. Yet to certain creatures, too much water means death and destruction. Nothing in the Multiverse is all positive (good, if you will) or all negative. It is a blend.

So forget all your preconceived ideas about Satan, Beelzebub, or whomever, because they don't exist. Unless they are demons masquerading as angels, in which case you zap them out of your vicinity or ground them in the earth to be bound and realigned. The best defense against demons happens to be angels. It would be a good guess to say that angels take great offense at demons pretending to be them. In modern terms, demons are attempting identity theft and con artistry.

Here is a beautiful example of how the Light and Shadow angels work harmoniously together to benefit this planet—and by doing so, influence and balance all levels and planets in the Multiverse. Each dawn, certain Light angels sing to the area of the earth where the sun rises. This reenergizes the planet. Since the sun is constantly rising somewhere, this song continuously fills the earth's atmosphere.

At each sunset, certain Shadow angels sing while the sun sets and the moon rises. This chant, which harmonizes with the Light angels' song, is also constant. These two angelic choirs provide balanced energy currents that sweep around the earth. The daily energy balance of this planet plays its part in the correct working of the Multiverse.

If you are using chants or prayers for angels, your work will be stronger if you call upon a Light angel and a Shadow angel, who both work in the same or similar areas of power. Chapters 5 and 6 have lists of these angels. Unless you plan to use the Combined Angels Ritual in chapter 7, you don't need to worry about casting a sacred protective circle. Calling upon a Shadow angel isn't going to hurt you, unless you have a negative result in mind, in which case (angels or not) you are likely to get your fingers burned.

My advice is to study slowly, make as many friends as you can among both Light and Shadow angels, and you will find spiritual doors opening that you never expected to see. All angels exist to help us grow spiritually and better understand the Supreme Power.

Before anyone jumps to a wrong conclusion, I am not, nor have I ever been, a Satanist. Satan isn't a personal name, anyway, as I have already discussed. Nor do I believe in the orthodox religions' idea of a devil. However, I do believe in the existence of evil. I just don't believe that evil has a mighty leader equal to the Goddess/God/Higher Power.

Not everyone will agree on the old knowledge I share in this book, particularly on the subject of angels. It may make many people uncomfortable to be confronted with such a drastic change in angelic descriptions. Some will reject it outright rather than consider that what they were taught was wrong. For others, a light will turn on in their minds, and they will benefit by incorporating the "new" ideas into their spiritual and magickal paths.

I hope each reader looks at all the material in each category with an open mind. Examining a subject from a new angle often reveals new doors and trains of thoughts. The Multiverse is full of mystical knowledge that we have yet to fully unravel. Some of what we think we know will be expanded upon. Completely new facts about the Otherworld realms will appear, as if out of nowhere, and take us by surprise. The mystics, spiritual alchemists, shamans, and other travelers who constantly seek wisdom will break the trail into new frontiers, as they did in the past in the fields of science, healing, astronomy, chemistry, geometry, and inventions.

Please explore the Nine Degrees of Light and Shadow, and the associated angels, with your mind open, expecting positive, exciting things, for these will happen. Enjoy this new look at ancient companions.

5. Light Angels

Nine Degrees of Light in the Otherworld

As you can see in the illustration on page 81, there are two separate columns (for lack of a better descriptive word) that rise parallel to each other, and above what we call the Highest of the Otherworld realms. One column is the Nine Degrees of Light, the other the Nine Degrees of Shadow. This area is accessible only to angels, those nonhuman beings who communicate directly with the Supreme Power. The angels' existence makes logical sense since the Supreme Power is too esoteric for humans to understand, thus making a direct connection with that Power nearly impossible.

The other reason for the angels is that the Supreme Power must lower its intensely high vibrations, in which positive and negative energies are melded together, through a series of steps until the duality needed for manifestation is reached.

The names I have used to designate the Nine Degrees will differ in some places from other "historical" lists. That shouldn't matter, as few of the other lists agree either.

Nine Degrees of Light

1. *Seraphim* (*seraph*, singular). Fire of Divine Love and Light. According to the Book of Enoch, there are four seraphim to match the four winds of the world. Enoch also describes them as having four faces and six wings each. The Prince of seraphim is variously named as Seraphiel or Jehoel. One source says seraphim roar like lions.

2. *Cherubim* (*cherub*, singular). The Wheels, the Strong Ones, Flames of Whirling Swords. In the ancient Akkadian language, this means "one who prays or intercedes." Assyrian, Chaldean, and Babylonian art portray the cherubim as huge winged bulls or sphinxes with human heads (sometimes called the Sheddim). The book of Ezekiel says they each have four faces and four wings. Their chief ruler's name depends upon what you read: Ophaniel, Rikbiel, Cherubiel, Zophiel, Raphael, or Gabriel.

3. *Bene Erelim*. The Thrones, the Valiant Ones, Chariots of God, the Many-Eyed Ones, Sons of God. They constantly sing the praises of the Supreme Power. Their leader is listed as Azazel or Hofniel.

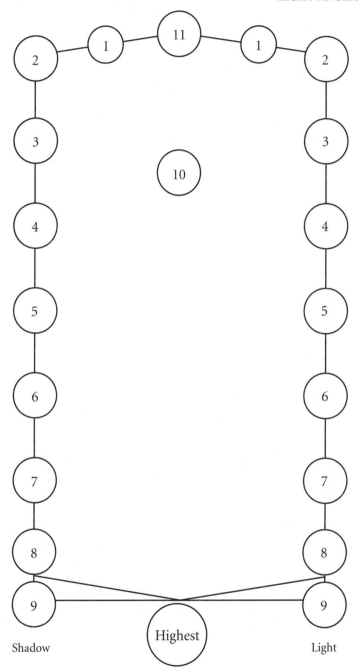

Nine Degrees of Light and Shadow

4. *Hashmallim*. Dominions, the Brilliant Ones, Mercy. Their leader is Hashmal, Zadkiel, or Zacharael. The hashmallim are said to carry or support the foundation of the Supreme Being. Since this doesn't really make sense, they more likely form the descending manifestational power into a more usable state.

5. *Tarshishim*. The Virtues, the Shining Ones, the Kings. They are usually shown as a group of twelve or more. Their ruling princes are listed as Barbiel, Uzziel, Peliel, Michael, and Raphael. Miracles, magick, grace, and valor.

6. *Ischim*. Souls of Flame, the Powers. Chief of this Degree is Azazel. Warriors of all spiritual enemies.

7. *Nations*. Principalities, the Archons. They are assigned to certain earthly nations and cities to help leaders make the right decisions. Among the names of their leaders are Requel, Haniel, and Cerviel. They are great cosmic forces that interact with this world.

8. *Archangels*. The Holy Ones, the Princes. These are the chief messengers of the Supreme Power and, although confusingly listed in this position, are the most powerful of angels. There are four Chief Princes: Michael, Gabriel, Raphael, and Uriel. However, other texts list Azrael (angel of death), Israfel (angel of music or Judgment trumpets), Raguel, Seraqael, Baracheil, Jehudiel, Sealtiel, Oriphiel, Zadkiel, Ratziel, Tzaphqiel, Tzadqiel, Khamael, Metatron, and Haniel. They are the supervisors of guardian angels and seem to have the last word on orders from the Supreme Power to all other angels. The Roman Catholic Church elevated Michael, Gabriel, and Raphael to sainthood.

9. *Angels*. The Carriers of Prayers. This may appear to be the lowest rank of angels, but they work the closest with humans as mediators and ministers over the natural world. Guardian angels come from this Degree; Light and Shadow guardian angels work together with each person. The study of angels is called *angelology*. According to ancient Jewish mysticism, there are nine female angels, who preside over a place called Women's Paradise. There are more angels of this working class than of any other kind.

Between both columns lies the Gate of Balance. This is called the *Abyss* by the Light angels and the *Brilliant Height* by the Shadow angels. It is a spiritual connecting door between both sets of angelic Degrees. This Gate is ruled by Zagzagel (Divine Splendor), the Angel of Wisdom. He is a Prince of the Presence, a teacher of angels, and one who speaks all languages of the Multiverse. Tradition says that Zagzagel is an angel of the Nations.

Above the two columns of Nine Degrees are three uninhabited levels, areas of power emanating from the Supreme Power as it gradually lowers its vibrations to duality. These three areas above the Nine Degrees of Light are called (lowest to highest): *Absolute Void*, *Boundless Infinity*, and *Limitless Light*.

The Nine Degrees of Light are meant to be a map to help humans understand, in some small way, the great depth and diversity of the Otherworld. It can also be a personal map or plan to chart your own spiritual progress. You have to understand that extremely few humans will reach the perfect balance. We spend lifetimes in a dance that moves us closer to perfection for a few seconds, then takes us away. We cannot remain in a physical body once we reach the balance, or Golden Mean.

Light Angels

The main problem in writing about angels has been the lack of correct information and translations of ancient texts. To my astonishment, this was remedied by several well-known professors in the mid-1990s. These new translations from original material should have created some rethinking. However, as is unfortunately common with drastic changes, the controversial subject was buried.

I've been asked to write about angels before, but I refused on the grounds that I felt something was missing from the truth in the available information. I came across too many conflicting statements in my reading. And for some reason, all the books written about angels portrayed them in what I call the fluff-bunny image, which certainly doesn't fit many of them and their recorded behavior. The new translations put all angels, both the Light and the Shadow angels, in a whole new context. Placing these classifications against what I already knew about the Multiverse and the way it operates solidified some information I had and completely changed other ideas I had about angels.

It is an interesting experience to keep a journal of your interaction with angels. It isn't uncommon to find small, fluffy, white feathers when you work with these angelic beings. Obviously, angels don't have feathers; this is merely their way of showing you they are around. Put the feathers on your angel altar; if you have pets, place the feathers in a box. Angels speak to us in dreams, meditations, and sometimes just by a sudden unexpected flow of thoughts in our minds. By writing all this down in a private journal, you will have a wonderful record of your progress.

Following is a list of Light angels and their principal working powers and areas of expertise. By no means is this list complete. Since the number of angels en masse is unknown, no list can possibly ever be complete.

List of Light Angels

Ariel: Lioness of God. Also called Arael, Ariael, or Arial. Color: pale pink. Stone: rose quartz. She helps with confidence, courage, bravery, and focus. Heals and protects nature and all wild creatures.

Azrael: Whom God Helps. Also called Azrail, Ashriel, or Azaril. Color: creamy vanilla. Stone: light yellow calcite. As the gentle angel of death, she helps people pass over without suffering. Also sends healing energy to those who grieve.

Baradiel: An archangel who rules over hail and other negative weather.

Cassiel: Angel of Solitude and Tears. Also called Casiel, Casziel, or Kafziel. Planet: Saturn. Day: Saturday (along with Machatan and Uriel). Dragons, temperance.

Chamuel: He Who Seeks God; an archangel. Also called Camuael, Camuel, Kamuel, Khamael, or Simiel. Planet: Mars. Color: light green. Stone: green fluorite. Helps find lost objects or people. Strengthens relationships, seeks out proper mate. Can open doors to a new or better career. Helps you become centered and calm.

Gabriel: God is My Strength; feminine. Prince of Change and Alteration. Element: Water. Planet: the moon. Zodiac: Cancer, Scorpio, Pisces. Incense: lavender. He is a messenger. Colors: orange, blue, golden yellow. Stone: citrine. Mercy, birth, hope. Brings new beginnings, psychic powers, and visions. Protects and gives you power to nurture yourself. Television and radio work, artists, writers, journalists.

Haniel: Glory of God; Grace of God. She is also called Anael, Onoel, Aniel. Planet: Venus. Zodiac: Capricorn. Month: December. Color: bluish-white. Stone: moonstone. Astrology, astronomy, moon energy, divination, spiritual healing, recover lost healing secrets. Helps with self-confidence.

Jeremiel: An archangel; Mercy of God, or Whom God Sets Up. Also known as Ramiel or Remiel. Color: dark purple. Stone: amethyst. Heals imbalances in life or helps you change them. Promotes psychic dreams and understanding of them.

Jophiel: Beauty of God; seems feminine. Also called Iofiel and Zophiel. Color: rose pink. Stone: rose quartz, pink rubellite. Helps to clear out clutter and interferences from your life. Aids creativity of any kind. Teaches you to release stress and slow down.

Kiramull Katibin: The two guardian angels in Arabic. One stands on the right side to contemplate and advise, the other on the left to record all deeds.

Malkiel: God's King. Also called Malchiel. Angelic guard of the South Wind.

Metatron: Prince of Countenances, Angel of the Covenant, Prince of Ministering Angels. Also called Metratton, Mittron, Metaraon, or Merraton. Element: elusive Spirit, or the center; this also includes all angels. Planet and zodiac: all signs and planets. Incense: lotus. Color: gold, silver. Stone: watermelon tourmaline. Brings spiritual development and mystical illumination. Teaches the use of sacred geometry.

Organization and record-keeping skills. Manifests all needs used for working with children.

Michael: He Who Is Like God, Prince of Splendor and Wisdom, Disperser of the Forces of Darkness. Also called Sabbathiel, Mika'il, or Beshter. Element: Fire. Planet: sun. Zodiac: Aries, Leo, Sagittarius. Incense: cinnamon. Shown wearing armor and carrying a sword. Colors: red, green, royal blues and purples. Stone: sugalite. A warrior angel associated with justice. Loyalty, defense, protection. Protector of police officers and firefighters. Use to cut all inappropriate psychic and physical links with others and also when under psychic attack. Brings courage, protection, and problem-solving. Clears all blockages of any type.

Raguel: Friend of God. Also called Akrasiel, Rasuil, or Suryan. Archangel of justice and fairness, helps oversee all angels. Color: very pale blue. Stone: aquamarine. Works for the underdog. Resolves conflicts, disputes, arguments. Helps you to see past illusions and trickery.

Raphael: Prince of Brightness, Beauty, and Life. Originally called Labbiel by the Chaldeans. One of the Holy Watchers. Element: Air. Planet: Mercury. Zodiac: Libra, Aquarius, Gemini. Incense: carnation. Carries a caduceus. Angel of any in the medical and healing professions. Colors: yellow, violet. Stone: emerald, malachite. Healer of the world and humankind. Creativity, harmony. Call upon for healing work (especially mental healing), illness. After a psychic attack, call upon Raphael and Michael together. Reduces stress and anxiety, and also cravings and addictions. Helps you release old negative habits and patterns. Powerful healer of animals.

Raziel: Secret of God, Angel of Supreme Mysteries. Also called Ratziel, Suriel, Akrasiel, Gallizur, or Saraqael. Color: all true colors. Stone: clear quartz crystals. Can help you to understand all esoteric knowledge, manifestation rules, sacred geometry, quantum physics, and higher levels of psychic abilities.

Sahaqiel: Angelic ruler of the sky. Element: Air.

Sandalphon: Angel of Glory, Angel of Prayer. Also called Sandolphon or Sandolfon. Color: turquoise. Stone: turquoise. Carries all prayers straight to the Supreme Power and returns the answers as soft as feathers. Music. Battles all evil constantly.

Sarakika'il: Arabic name of the Prince of the Council of Judging Angels. Zodiac: Aries. Mercy, guidance, releasing negative habits.

Shufiel: Grouped with Michael and Gabriel as a spell-binding angel.

Tsadkiel: Angel of Justice; Kaddisha, the Holy One. Also called Tzadquel, Tzadkiel, or Azza. Helps guard the gate of the East Wind. Planet: Jupiter. Helps you gain intelligence and knowledge.

Tzaphquiel: Contemplation of God. Also called Tzaphkiel. Planet: Saturn. Helps you learn the listening process of meditation.

Uriel: Prince of Knowledge and Truth, Fire of God. Element: Earth. Planet: Venus. Zodiac: Capricorn, Taurus, Virgo. Incense: musk. Colors: shades of brown, black, silver, and green. Stone: amber. Carries a scroll. Intuition, mystery. Brings teaching, insight, and stability. Gives warnings and prophecies. Helps with studies and tests. Divine magick, recovery from natural disasters, pours light on cloudy situations to reveal the truth.

Vngsursh: Angel of the summer solstice. Call upon Vngsursh for protection against ill-wishing and curses.

Zadkiel: Righteousness of God. Also called Satqiel, Tzadkiel, or Zidekiel. An archangel of benevolence and mercy. Color: deep indigo. Stone: lapis lazuli. Call upon Zadkiel, along with Michael, to nullify negative energies. Cleans out emotional debris from the heart chakra. Helps with memory and has access to all knowledge. Helps you find lost objects, improve on studies and tests, and develop compassion for yourself and others.

Having presented all these traditional but hard-to-pronounce names, I'll let you in on a little secret about angels that makes quick petitions a lot easier. You don't have to memorize tongue-twisting names to get immediate, or nearly so, results. Just ask help from the Angel of Parking Spaces, the Angel of Easy Travel, the Angel of Finding the Right Help, and so on. Just ask for the angel of whatever you need is, and you will be amazed at the immediate aid that comes your way, the unexpected doors that open to fill your request.

Sometimes the requests we have to make are very difficult ones, but the answers always come, filled with love. Often we get the answers in dreams, which is why we should pay attention to all our dreams. You will know instinctively when a dream is an answer, or whether it is just your subconscious mind sorting out weird daily garbage. Answers sent by angels through dreams are most definitely not like other dreams.

In 2002, my husband, Charles, had been ill with terminal cancer (everywhere in his body) for two years. It never occurred to me that I wouldn't care for him by myself. I just adjusted my thinking and did what had to be done because our love was so great. The doctors had told us in July 2000 that he would only live two or three more months, but our combined strength gave him two years.

However, by mid-April 2002, when the cancer was everywhere, including six brain tumors, I realized that soon he would have to be drugged into unconsciousness to endure the pain. I did the hardest thing then that I ever had to do in my life—I released him completely into the hands of the Goddess. My prayer was: "The best birthday present you could give me this year is that Charles doesn't have to suffer anymore."

Early the next morning, I had a vivid dream in color and with total sound. When I have dreams such as that one, I know they are prophetic. I stood in the Otherworld overlooking a great meadow that stretched as far as I could see. Behind me were the beautiful, white stone columns of an open temple. People of every race, culture, and religion stood in that meadow, filling it end to end. From out of the open temple came hundreds of angels—singing, dancing, and shaking tambourines. The song they sang is forever in my memory, both the words and music; I later wrote it down. I watched as the waiting crowd took up the beautiful, happy song until the Otherworld rang with their joy.

I was sitting up in bed when I woke, crying in hysterical sobs that I couldn't stop. There had been nothing negative about the dream—in fact, just the opposite. But I knew in my heart that the angels were waiting for Charles to make his journey to join them very soon. I had the blankets muffling my sobs as I heard Charles getting his coffee in the kitchen. I ran into the bathroom, shut the door, and stuffed a towel in my mouth so he wouldn't hear. I crouched on the floor in a corner for over an hour before I could gain control.

No amount of cold water could hide the fact that my eyes were red and swollen, so I got dressed and went to sit with Charles. He looked at me and said, "Did you dream about me?" I told him no, I had dreamed about singing angels. He smiled and said, "It will be okay. I just worry about leaving you alone."

Ten days later, on my birthday, I sat beside his bed where he lay drugged unconscious, and told him that it was all right for him to leave with his spirit guides, whom I could see in the room. That I would be fine. That the guides and angels had a big welcome party waiting for him. He peacefully died in his sleep a few hours later.

However, I was never alone for the next three years. Eight months after Charles journeyed to the Otherworld, I had a sudden heart attack and stroke. With my low cholesterol and blood pressure, the event took all the doctors, and me, by surprise. I went through the heart attack alone, lying in bed one night. The only symptom I had was a pain in my left arm from shoulder to fingertips. I felt myself slipping away, and saw a brilliantly lighted gate before me. I headed straight for that gate but was immediately stopped by two very large angels, glowing with light.

"You have to go back," they said. Being as stubborn as I am, I said no, and tried to get around them. "You can't come now," they repeated. "You have to go back." And with that, they shoved me back into my body. Although I was drenched in perspiration, the terrible ripping pain was gone from my left arm. I felt the bed beside me move and knew Charles was with me. I still waited until morning before I called the ambulance.

For three years after that, and after a miraculous recovery, I daily heard the kitchen door open; Charles's footsteps cross the linoleum to his chair; and the low, almost out-of-earshot sound of his voice. The cats would prick up their ears and run to join him. I knew if I entered the room, I couldn't touch him, so I just sat and listened. Suddenly, his visits stopped without warning in the fall of 2005. I didn't know until later that was the time Charles made an appearance in, and saved the life of, a man who would soon come into my life.

When the daily visits from Charles ended, I felt lost. Angrily, I voiced my complaint to the angels. Where were they when I needed comfort? Why didn't they show me signs of their presence? Other people were gifted with fluffy feathers as a sign of angelic presence. Why didn't the angels give me at least one small feather? Thank goodness that angels are compassionate and understanding, because I wasn't very polite.

Then, on a very rainy November day in 2005, I went out to fill the bird feeders as I always do during the winter months. While I filled the feeders, there was nothing on that wet, green grass except raindrops. But when I turned to go back inside, I saw a tiny, white, dry feather on the grass in front of me. As I carefully picked up one, another would appear nearby out of thin air, until I discovered there were a total of nine. Not only that, but each white feather had a thin line of dark gray up the center. If it had been spring, I would have put the incident down as baby-bird feathers, but that isn't possible in November. Nor could I explain why they were all totally dry in the pouring rain, and all lying in one little area.

So the angels answered my complaint with a little humor. The gray line represented the presence of the Shadow angels combined with the white of the Light angels. Then I realized that there had been minor occurrences of angelic presence before; I simply hadn't paid attention. I called upon the parking space angel and the traffic-light angel frequently, but I had forgotten to thank them for their help. Another great helper had been the Angel of Loud-Music Neighbors. I had stopped looking for the tiny daily miracles, not a wise thing to do.

Angels are everywhere, waiting for us to ask for help. They aren't allowed to interfere with our life plan, and usually don't give aid unless asked. However, they will suddenly appear, seen or unseen, in emergencies or potential disasters. They take the form of a human you never see again, or who vanishes as soon as you are out of danger. Angels can come to you at any time, so be aware.

Saints and Fabled Members of the White Lodge

Humans who have been declared saints by churches, and other humans who are wise members of the Otherworld's White Lodge (sometimes called the White Brotherhood), are often called upon for help. Although upon reading most of the so-called lives of the saints, anyone can see that these people either never actually lived, or the stories of their lives have been greatly exaggerated. Some of the humans listed we know lived selfless lives of love and did many good deeds—not because they had to, but because they felt it was the right thing to do. A fine example of this is Mother Teresa of India. However, the very act of believing in, and calling upon, these saints have built up a spiritual reservoir of power in the Otherworld, powers that respond to our requests.

The Second Vatican Council of the Catholic Church, in their Constitution on the Church (*Lumen Gentium*), number 50, stated that saints are helpful friends to whom one could show devotion, but not worship. These devotions usually consist of saying prayers, lighting candles, and offering flowers or incense.

Two stones listed in modern books on stones are specifically mentioned as aids to reaching saints and ascended members of the White Lodge: moldavite and tanzanite. However, both stones are expensive and often difficult to find. If you want to use a stone on your altar when you talk to the saints or ascended teachers, quartz crystal will work just fine.

List of Saints and Ascended Teachers

Agabus, Saint: Patron of psychics and clairvoyant visions

Agatha, Saint: Breast diseases, rape, volcanic eruptions. Patroness of nurses.

Agnes, Saint: Fidelity, finding a suitable mate, help with relationships

Agricola of Avignon, Saint: Protection against misfortune, bad luck, and plagues. Patron of rain.

Albinus, Saint: Gallstones and kidney diseases

Alexis, Saint: Keeping away enemies

Alodia and Nunilo, Saints: Patronesses of child-abuse victims and runaways

Aloysius, Saint: Fever, epidemics, plagues; settling disputes

Alphonsus Liguori, Saint: Rheumatic fever, arthritis in any form; gout, joint, and muscle ailments

Andrew, Saint: Patron of fishermen

Ann, Saint: Help with deafness and blindness, and with special requests. Patroness of women, particularly those in childbirth.

Anthony, Saint: Finding lost items. Marriage or love problems, financial problems, getting a job. Considered a wonder-worker.

Apollonia, Saint: Patron of toothaches and dentists

Arthelius, Saint: Patroness of kidnapping victims

Babaji: A yogi known as "The Deathless Avatar" and the teacher of Paramahansa Yogananda. Yoga, enlightenment, meditation, spiritual growth.

Barbara, Saint: Protectress of women. Love, help against those trying to break up a marriage. Clear a path through obstacles; drive away evil; release from prison. Patroness of prisoners, architects, the military, and stoneworkers.

Bartholomew, Saint: Learn the truth. Protect from violence. Patron of surgeons.

Benedict, Saint: Fever, kidney disease, poisons, contagious diseases, sick animals. Safe delivery in childbirth. Business success. Protection from storms.

Bernardine of Siena, Saint: Gambling addictions

Blaise, Saint: Diseases in both humans and animals, especially throat diseases. Patron of veterinarians.

Brigid of Kildare, Saint: Healing, childbirth, fertility, agriculture, love. Knowledge, poetry, prophecy, inspiration. Protection from fires. Patroness of blacksmiths, dairy workers, and physicians.

Cadoc of Wales, Saint: Glandular disorders

Capistrano, Saint: Repelling enemies

Catherine of Alexandria, Saint: Beauty, fertility, love, fortunate birth. A peaceful death. Visions and dreams; public speaking. Patroness of teachers and jurors.

Catherine of Siena, Saint: Patroness of nursing homes and unmarried women. Protection from fire.

Cecilia, Saint: Success in composing music. Poets and singers.

Christopher, Saint: Protection from accidents and sudden death. Safe travel. Fevers, storms, nightmares. Patron of unmarried men, bus drivers, motorists, and travelers of all kinds.

Ciprano, Saint: Protection while traveling. Keeping out of jail. Repels bad neighbors, liars, and deceitful lovers. Homeless people; earthquakes, fire.

Clare of Assisi, Saint: Overcoming drug and alcohol problems. Help with difficulties and understanding.

Clotilde, Saint: Adopted children and widows

Cosmas and Damian, Saints: Correct diagnosis of diseases, sickness. Removing obstacles. Patrons of barbers, druggists, physicians, surgeons.

Denis, Saint: Headaches

Dismas, Saint: Patron of prisoners, thieves, death-row inmates, undertakers

Dymphna, Saint: Nervous disorders, any mental problems. Family harmony. Epilepsy, seizures.

El Morya: Lived as Ranbir Singh, a member of the royal family of Kashmir in the 1800s. Protection and assistance in any legal or political situation.

Elmo, Saint: Appendicitis, intestinal disease, seasickness

Expedite, Saint: Settling disputes and changing things quickly

Fabiola, Saint: Infidelity, physical abuse. Patroness of divorce and widows.

Florian, Saint: Protecting the home against fire and flood. Helping in danger and emergencies. Patron of firefighters.

Francis de Sales, Saint: Deafness. Patron of writers and journalists.

Francis of Assisi, Saint: Born to a wealthy Italian cloth merchant, he began the Franciscan Order. Understanding, peace, spiritual wisdom, help with problems. Patron of all animals and birds, the environment, gardens, firefighters, merchants, and garment-makers.

Francis Xavier Cabrini, Saint: The poor, being accepted when you move. Health, education. Patron of emigrants.

George, Saint: Courage, conquering fear, overcoming jealousy. Skin diseases, mental retardation. Patron of soldiers.

Gerard Majella, Saint: Pregnant women, mothers with small children, healing, seeing the truth. Protection from false accusations. Prophecy.

Gertrude of Nivelles, Saint: Getting rid of mice and rats. Patroness of cats.

Giles, Saint: Patron of the physically disabled

Helen of Jerusalem, Saint: Love, overcoming sorrow. Patroness of archaeologists.

Hilarion: A fourth-century Middle Easterner renowned for healing. Healing, clearing of energy.

Hippolytus, Saint: Patron of horses

Hubert, Saint: Patron of dogs, hunters, and those who suffer from rabies

Ignatius of Loyola, Saint: Protection from burglars and evil spirits. Patron of soldiers.

Infant Jesus of Prague: Health matters, surgery, guidance, wisdom

James the Greater, Saint: Conquering enemies. Removal of obstacles, finding justice. Arthritis, rheumatism. Patron of manual laborers.

Joan of Arc, Saint: Courage, spiritual strength, overcoming enemies

John Bosco, Saint: Temporal needs, students, troublesome children. Patron of editors.

John Gualbert, Saint: Patron of foresters and park services

John the Baptist, Saint: Good luck, protection from enemies. Patron of tailors.

John the Divine, Saint: Friendship. Patron of art dealers, editors, and publishers.

Joseph, Saint: Protection, finding a job, selling a house, married couples. Patron of carpenters and bakers.

Jude, Saint: Hopeless cases, court trouble, or getting out of jail. Drug addiction.

King Solomon: Hebrew king. Spiritual alchemy, building new projects, resolving dilemmas.

Kuthumi (sometimes spelled **Koot Hoomi**): Brought to notice by Helena Blavatsky, Kuthumi is a Sikh spiritual leader named Sirdar Thakar Singh Sadhanwali who lived in India during the 1800s. Motivation, focusing on priorities, finding your life purpose.

Lady Nada: Mentioned as working with Saint-Germain. Balancing female and male energies.

Lawrence, Saint: Peaceful home and family. Financial assistance. Patron of the poor.

Lazarus, Saint: Sickness, diseases of the legs, drug addiction. Prosperity.

Leonard, Saint: Burglary, prisoners of war, women in labor

Louis Bertrand, Saint: Protection from evil and accidents. Learning languages.

Lucy, Saint: Eye diseases. Help when your back is against the wall. Repelling legal problems, settling court cases. Repelling hexes and curses. Patroness of salespeople and writers.

Luke, Saint: Patron of painters, physicians, and surgeons

Mahachohan Ragoczy (pronounced *Maw-how-ko-han Rag-ok-see*): Said to be a great spiritual teacher of Saint-Germain. Esoteric learning. Guides world leaders toward peace.

Martha, Saint: Domestic problems, money trouble, keeping a lover or husband faithful. Finding a new love. Conquering enemies. Patroness of housekeepers and servants.

Martin de Porres, Saint: Financial needs, health, harmony. Patron of the poor and animals.

Martin of Tours, Saint: Repelling evil, protecting from enemies. Money, good luck, a successful business.

Mary Magdalene, Saint: Patroness of repentant prostitutes. Also perfume-makers and hair stylists.

Matthew, Saint: Patron of bankers, bookkeepers, customs agents, security guards, and tax collectors

Melchizedek: Canaanite priest-king and teacher of the biblical Abraham. Sacred geometry, manifestation.

Michael, Archangel: Total protection. Patron of police officers.

Mother Mary: Intercedes for anyone asking help, mercy, or any need. Helps children and their caretakers. Love, kindness, protection.

Mother Teresa of Calcutta: A twentieth-century nun who dedicated her life to working with the poor and dying people in India.

Our Lady of Fatima: Protection from evil and the anger of adversaries. Freedom from any situation that restricts and binds.

Our Lady of Guadelupe: Peace, sickness, luck. Help in any situation.

Our Lady of Loretto: Help when looking for a place to live; protection when traveling by air. Peace in the family. Patroness of pilots and home builders.

Our Lady of Lourdes: Sickness, regaining health

Our Lady of Mercy: Peace, health, justice, release from jail

Our Lady of Mount Carmel: Protection from accidents or sudden death

Our Lady of the Immaculate Conception: Sickness, fertility

Paramahansa Yogananda: Born in India but taught self-realization in the United States. Yoga, developing meditation skills.

Patrick, Saint: Prosperity, good luck, spiritual wisdom, guidance. Protection against snakebites.

Paul the Venetian: The Italian Renaissance artist Paolo Caliari of Verona during the 1500s. Artistic talents, freeing creativity.

Paul, Saint: Courage, overcoming opposition, a peaceful home. Patron of authors, journalists, publishers, and travelers.

Peregrine Laziosi, Saint: Health problems, especially cancer

Peter, Saint: Success, good business, strength, courage, good luck, removal of obstacles. Patron of bridge-builders and masons.

Philomena, Saint: Fertility, pregnant women, destitute mothers, trouble with children, happiness in the home. Mental illness, money problems, real estate. Patroness of any desperate situation.

Raymond Nonnatus, Saint: Stopping gossip, protecting unborn babies. Patron of midwives.

Rita of Cascia, Saint: Repelling evil and abusive relationships. Marital problems, infertility, parenthood. Loneliness, healing wounds and tumors, bleeding. Patroness of hopeless cases and desperate situations.

Saint-Germain: A count who gave gems and life-elixirs to friends. Music, languages, honesty in government, world peace. Helps all earthly Light Workers; Light Workers are those who study and teach to keep spiritual truths alive.

Sebastian, Saint: Justice, court cases, removal of obstacles. Overcoming rivals. Obtaining good fortune. Patron of athletes, gardeners, potters, stonemasons, soldiers.

Serapis Bey: Origins seem to be connected to Egypt. Motivation to take action.

Siddhartha Gautama Buddha: India. Developing meditation. Overcoming any suffering or adversity.

Teresa of Ávila, Saint: Headaches, heart attacks, strokes

Thérèse of Lisieux, Saint: Alcohol and drug problems, tuberculosis. Spiritual growth. Protect against ill-wishing and black magick.

Thomas Aquinas, Saint: Improving memory, passing school tests. Patron of scholars and students.

Vitus, Saint: Curing epilepsy, exorcising evil spirits. Patron of comedians and dancers.

Working with Light Angels

When working with either Light or Shadow angels, you should do so with great respect. Even Light angels are very powerful and can be literal to the point of danger. That is why it is best to work with both a Light and a Shadow angel at the same time.

Often, the best results come from writing out requests in the Celestial or Angelic alphabet, shown in the illustration on the next page. You can petition an angel according to purpose, day, month, planet, or zodiac sign.

The uses of magickal alphabets originated with the Arabs during the Middle Ages, when they were renowned as magicians. Western Europe learned these alphabets when the Arabs conquered Spain. Toledo, Spain had, at the time, the only university that taught magick and sorcery. The Arabs called these magickal scripts *rihani* (magick) because of the power they contained.

However, one of the most famous alphabets—the Enochian, or Angelic—came through the angelic work of Dr. John Dee and Edward Kelley in England. Dee (1527–1608) was an astrologer, mathematician, and English spy during the reign of Queen Elizabeth I.

By writing out a petition using the Angelic alphabet, you are focusing your intentions toward the manifestation of your desire. All of your energy is placed in that direction, and positive results are inevitable. Although angels can work to keep you safe and on your path, they are not allowed to intervene in your life without your permission. For all those people who insist that we must suffer and struggle to grow, I have great news. We can grow faster through peacefulness.

Write out your petition on a piece of paper while burning a candle of a corresponding request color. Speak to the angel

Celestial or Angelic Alphabet

A	B	D	G
H	I	K	L
M	N	O	P
Q	R	S	T
V	Z	CH	SH
TH	TZ		

or angels as you would to a good friend; angels are not to be worshiped. Do a mental cleansing, perhaps followed by a short meditation. Then light the folded paper in the candle flame. Drop it into a metal bowl to burn. Thank the angels to whom you have sent the petition.

If you are afraid of asking for the wrong thing, at the end of your petition, write: "This, or something better."

Although certain stones are listed with some angels, traditions tie other stones to all angels. These stones are: quartz crystal, apophyllite, selenite, purple fluorite, blue celestite, blue chalcedony, ametrine, kunzite, danburite, elestial crystal, seraphinite, amethyst, and Herkimer diamonds. However, if you can't afford, or find, these, you can use clear quartz crystal to represent Light angels and elestial crystal or smoky quartz to represent Shadow angels.

Candle Colors for All Angels

Black: Absorbs or repels evil magick and energies, ill-wishing, even thought forms. Can bind, protect, and break barriers.

Blue, light: Inspiration, knowledge, finding the truth, good health, harmony

Blue, royal: Group success, developing psychic power

Brown: Attracts opportunities for financial success. Intuition, study.

Gold: Good luck, quick money, change of luck, gaining knowledge. Peaceful work with those in authority.

Green: Very good to settle an unstable situation. Abundance, material gain, marriage, fresh outlook on life, new beginnings.

Indigo or turquoise: Neutralizes evil magick. Stops gossip and lies. Balances karma.

Magenta, cranberry, or maroon: Burn with other colors for fast results and quick changes.

Orange: Quickly change your luck. Creativity, prosperity, energy. Encourages study.

Pink: Spiritual awakening, friends, healing. Attracts gentle love.

Purple: Removes curses and bad luck. Drives away evil. Breaks anyone's control over you. Rapid transformations.

Red: Counters psychic attack. Potency in attraction. Energy, willpower, good health.

Silver or light gray: Neutralizes any unpleasant situation. Repels stress and bothersome people. Good for meditation.

White: When in doubt about a color, use white. Contacts angels.

Yellow: Creativity, mental clarity, business ventures, confidence. Helps with the study of any kind of healing.

Light-Angel Oil

Use a small dark bottle with a lid. Pour in one-fourth of a teaspoon of pure almond oil as a base. Add one drop each of the following oils: lotus, rose, jasmine, honeysuckle, and wisteria. Rub this on any candles you burn for Light angels. You may also want to sprinkle holy water (see page 33) around the candles and/or your meditation area whenever you work there.

Angels of the Zodiac

Aries: Malkiel

Taurus: Asmodel

Gemini: Ambriel

Cancer: Muriel

Leo: Verchiel

Virgo: Hamaliel

Libra: Uriel

Scorpio: Barbiel

Sagittarius: Adnachiel

Capricorn: Haniel

Aquarius: Gabriel

Pisces: Barakiel

Angels of the Months

January: Gabriel

February: Barakiel

March: Malkiel

April: Asmodel

May: Ambriel

June: Muriel

July: Verchiel

August: Hamaliel

September: Uriel or Auriel

October: Barbiel

November: Adnachiel

December: Haniel

Angels of the Days of the Week

Monday: Gabriel

Tuesday: Camael

Wednesday: Michael

Thursday: Tzaphiel

Friday: Haniel

Saturday: Cassiel

Sunday: Raphael

Meeting the Five Major Archangels Meditation

The five major archangels are considered to be Michael, Gabriel, Raphael, Uriel, and Metatron. Traditionally, these archangels also represent the five commonly known elements of Air, Fire, Water, Earth, and Spirit.

Remember that you can always read the entire meditation onto an audiotape, leaving pauses in the places where you might want to explore more. Using a recorded tape also helps you relax more as you don't have to remember what comes next.

(Use the cleansing method mentioned on 16, and the meditation beginning practices listed on page 23.)

You are standing in a green meadow with a tall stone arch ahead of you. The area immediately around the arch is rocky and bare of vegetation. As you walk through the arch, you notice it is made of pale granite with tiny points of light sparkling deep inside the stone.

As you step through the arch to the other side, you find yourself in a desolate region—barren, rocky, and with great cracks in the ground. Out of these cracks come puffs of smoke followed by briefly leaping jets of flame. The flames rise so high at times that they fill the dark sky. You can feel the heated winds that flow from the flames, and you can hear the hiss and pop of the subterranean fires. As each jet of fire falls back into a crack, brilliant lightning shoots into the crevice from the black skies above.

You feel the power of the fires but are not afraid. You know you will be safe at all times. You are drawn to merge with the element of Fire. You want to experience the rise and fall of the energy, the tremendous potential for either destruction or creation. As you become one with the fire, you suddenly see the archangel Michael standing beside you. His eyes are like two fiery suns, while his robe is a white so brilliant that it is difficult to look at it. A golden breastplate of armor covers his torso. In one hand he holds a great sword entwined with flames.

You feel Michael's true nature as a spiritual but compassionate warrior as he looks deep into your eyes.

"Call upon me for courage, protection, justice, and help with solving problems," he says. Then he parts the surrounding flames with his sword. As if Michael had parted a curtain, you see an opening onto the cool shores of a deep mountain lake.

You walk through the opening, to stand with the blue-green waters of the lake lapping gently against your feet. In the night sky above, you see a full moon and feel the lunar pull coming to you from the water. You decide to experience the element of Water as part of yourself. You enter the lake and float peacefully and easily across the surface until you reach a tumbling stream that leaves the lake and heads toward the ocean. You continue to float down the stream, noticing the smaller streams that join with it to make a river. You sense the controlled power of the water as it smooths stones in its bed. You are aware of the many small life forms that the stream feeds and protects.

Suddenly, you become part of a waterfall that crashes downward, sending up clouds of mist and spray. A greater pull now moves you faster until you merge with an ocean. As you ride the waves, moonlight creating lights and shadows on the water, you begin to understand the influence of the moon on both oceanic tides and human lives.

As you rest in the gentle arms of the ocean, the archangel Gabriel appears. His blue robe ebbs and flows around him like the waves. His eyes remind you of deep, mysterious pools.

"Through me you can develop psychic power and visions," he tells you. As he points to the skies with one hand, you are drawn upward into storm clouds rolling in from the ocean.

You become aware of the great strength hidden in the element of Air as you let yourself become one with the storm. As with Fire and Water, you sense the power to create or destroy within the element of Air. You ride the winds over the coastline as heavy rains drench the land. The winds carry you on up into the high mountains beyond the ocean, where the rain turns to soft, cold snow. As the storm dips down the other side of the mountains, it softens into a warm breeze as it crosses a desert. Its passage shapes the grains of sand into elaborate patterns that remind you of ocean waves. You travel on until the breezes stir the tree branches of a woodland.

The archangel Raphael now rides the breeze at your side. His pale yellow robes flutter like bands of sunlight. Every breath of air moves his hair and makes it glow about his head.

"I teach the power of healing," he tells you as he gently touches your face. You feel healing power flow into you and through you into the earth below. Like a falling leaf, you spiral smoothly down until you merge with the element of Earth.

As you sink into the rich soil of the woodland, you become sensitive to all plant and animal life around you, as well as the ability to turn your awareness to other types of earth environment. You sense the dryness and the hidden fertility of the desert sands and how each oasis contributes to the desert life. The jungle feels steamy and rich with decaying tropical foliage, but it harbors an abundance of life.

"Listen," a soft voice says beside you. You become aware of the heartbeat of the earth as you turn to see the archangel Uriel, his green robe smelling of flowers and growing things. "I teach all things. I can help you learn insight and stability," he tells you. As you look into his golden eyes, you feel yourself being taken into the element of Spirit.

The tall archangel Metatron, dressed in dazzling white, awaits you on the rocky floor of a great cavern. The smooth walls are white with veins of pastel colors. This archangel leads you up a flight of stone stairs into a shaft of dazzling spiritual light. At the top, an open doorway stands between two pillars—one white, one black.

"In this sacred temple is the center of learning spiritual development and mystical illumination," Metatron tells you. "Sit on this bench patiently and listen." The archangel fades quickly from sight.

The scent of sweet incense floats through the air. Suspended from the ceiling is a huge silver star that flashes rays of light against the black walls and floor. The complete calm of the temple fills you, soothing your spirit of all cares and worries. You think about how all the elements you have seen and experienced have both the power to destroy or create. You begin to understand the balance and perfection of the Multiverse, and the part all beings play in that balance as they reach for personal perfection.

You hear faint angelic voices giving you messages. You will remember them. Then a puff of air blows incense smoke onto your face. You slide back into your physical body.

(End of meditation)

Angel Star Meditation

(Use the cleansing method mentioned on page 16, and the meditation beginning practices listed on page 23.)

You find yourself standing before the Golden Gate in the Upperworld. Through the glistening bars that form the gate, you can see the Goddess and the God sitting on separate thrones, as well as the extremely ancient dragon called She Who Sleeps.

Two shining angels come to greet you. You can see that their so-called wings are actually energy pouring out of their heart chakras and mixing with their brilliant auras near their shoulders. It is through this energy projection that angels can rapidly move. Each one in turn steps close to you and allows their wings to enfold you. You are filled with the knowledge that they will protect, love, and heal you without reservation.

Each angel takes you by the hand and instantly transports you into the velvet black skies of the Multiverse. You see thousands of brilliant stars and constellations that decorate the heavens. These celestial lights are brighter and clearer than you have ever seen them. This is because you are in deep space with no distracting reflections or energy waves to distort the pureness of their lights.

Each angel gently touches your heart chakra, clearing out blockages and opening it fully to the warm, spiritual love of the angels and the Supreme Power/Goddess/God. As this powerful, unconditional love fills your body, mind, and soul, you also feel your spirit aligning itself with certain star energies.

"You can renew this feeling and star connection any time by looking up at the night sky," the angels tell you.

"Even though the star flow will not be as strong during the day, it is still there for you."

One of the angels touches the center of your forehead. You feel a link being made between you and the stars that attracted you.

As you close your eyes, you feel yourself slipping back into your physical body.

(End of meditation)

Meeting Light Angels Meditation

Each archangel has an astral temple that is situated in the astral plane, that place between this world and the Otherworld. These are found above earthly sacred spots, many of which are unknown to present-day humans. This meditation will take you to a huge Light chamber where all Light angels can meet.

(Use the cleansing method mentioned on page 16, and the meditation beginning practices listed on page 23.)

You find your guardian angels beside you. They smile and reassure you of your complete safety as they swiftly take you from earth through a misty veil onto the astral plane. What appears as a gigantic, lighted crystal dome hangs in the heavens before you. The guardian angels, each holding your hands, join thousands of other angels who are entering this magnificent half-sphere. This is the Light chamber of the Light angels.

Although this bright chamber has angels moving about everywhere, you notice that there is more than enough room left to accommodate more angels than you could ever imagine. The presence of all these angelic beings produces dazzling patterns and arrays of colors. These constant light shows are accompanied by celestial music with singing in the angelic language. Other streams of music made visible come down from the planets and stars to mingle with the angels' songs.

You listen to the celestial music, feeling it fill your heart and soul with joy, until the spiritual song of your own individual being floats forth to join the choirs.

Each of the five major archangels (Michael, Gabriel, Raphael, Uriel, and Metatron) comes to you and places a secret spiritual symbol within your aura. This will enable you to call upon the archangels and their special powers and talents whenever you need. You probably will not recognize the sacred symbol immediately. However, when you have progressed along your path and are ready to learn about the symbol, you will recognize it and its importance to your growth.

You feel renewed and reenergized as your guardian angels return you to your physical body.

(End of meditation)

Chants and Petitions

Always believe in yourself and your goals. What we term miracles are simply universal laws we don't understand yet. And remember, what you build in your subconscious mind, or what some call imagination, is a channel of force. The more real it is to you, the more powerfully it works.

When you communicate with the angels, the saints, or the ascended teachers, you may always use your own words. Your subconscious mind will bring up the correct words to petition these beings for help, whether it be a physical, mental, emotional, or spiritual need. However, if you are timid at first, the following examples will help you gain self-confidence in the beginning.

Angel Chant

Goddess Version

(If you wish, you may rub angel oil on a white or colored candle to burn during your communication time.)

> *Angels of Light, who stand forever before the Goddess's power:*
>> *Hear the words and intent of my need in this hour.*
>> *Fulfill my request with understanding and love.*
>> *Know that I believe in the power from above.*

(State now what you desire to happen.)

>> *Bring this, or better.*

Pagan Version

(You may burn colored candles in a separate ritual, or combine this chant with a regular cast circle.)

> *Angels divine, who see and hear all*
> *Listen to my desire as I call*
> *To you for aid to fulfill*
> *My need according to my will.*

(State now what you desire to happen.)

> *Earth and Air combine, with Fire and Water, all divine.*
> *Entwine the energies with angelic power, and manifest the need within this hour.*

New Age Version

(As mentioned above, you may burn colored candles or decorate your altar with statues of angels. See the list of candle colors beginning on page 104. Add any feathers you might find. Sit or stand facing north as you say this chant.)

I call upon the archangel Raphael, who stands at my right hand. Fill me with potent words and ideas to fulfill my desire.

I call upon the archangel Michael, who stands behind him. Fill me with energy to grasp all opportunities that come my way.

I call upon the archangel Gabriel, who stands at my left hand. Fill my mind with correct intuition to know what is right for me and what is not.

I call upon the archangel Uriel, who stands before me. Ground me in practical earthly ways but teach me to reach to the Supreme Power for the miracles that will come.

(State your desire at this time.)

I thank you, archangels all, who came to help me at my call.

Chant to the Saints

As with angels, saints and ascended teachers are not to be worshiped. They are asked to help and intercede so that your desires may be fulfilled. You can choose one particular saint or ascended teacher, or you may call upon them all at the same time.

Goddess Version

All you saints and ascended ones, who are of and one with the Goddess from the beginning of the ancient days, I come to you with a request and need. (State what you desire.) *I ask that my need be made manifest. If this is not to be, please send me a message to explain. I feel this need deep within my being. Please fulfill my desire as I ask, or fulfill the need with something better. Thank you.*

Pagan Version

I call upon the ancient wise ones, who now dwell in the Otherworld realms. I have a desire that I wish to manifest in my life. (State what your desire is.) *I ask that all those with the power and wisdom to fulfill this desire, come to my aid. Lead me to the right paths and opportunities so that I may add to your efforts. Whisper to me messages that will guide my actions. So shall it be.*

I call Earth to bind my spell. Air to speed its travel well. Bright as Fire shall it glow. Deep as tide of Water flow.

Count the elements fourfold, and in the fifth the spell shall hold.

So mote it be.

New Age Version

(Choose a colored candle that represents the need you wish fulfilled. Or choose a color that represents a particular saint or ascended teacher. Light the candle before the chant, and extinguish it when you finished. You may wish to do a short meditation after the chant.)

I believe in the power of miracles, that the energy that produces miracles is alive and active in the Multiverse. I believe you have the wisdom to weave that energy into a form that will fulfill my desire. (State your desire.) *I humbly ask that you aid me in this request that my life may be better. Amen.*

6. Shadow Angels

Nine Degrees of Shadow in the Otherworld

The Nine Degrees of Shadow, the Otherworld realm of the Shadow angels, balances the Nine Degrees of Light of the Light angels. See the illustration on page 81. The two angelic realms are parallel to each other, as they rise above the Otherworld area called the Highest; the angelic energies finally merge into the pre-duality stages that lead to the Supreme Power.

The two realms of angels perfectly balance the energies that stream down from the Supreme Power, separating the energies into the duality of positive and negative. It is necessary to have both sets of energy vibrations for the manifestation of anything in the Multiverse—in fact, for the existence of the Multiverse itself. Like recipes, different mixtures of positive and negative energies are necessary to manifest different types of objects and beings. Therefore, it is vital for duality to be in existence.

If you study both lists of the Nine Degrees, you will notice that they complement each other. There is never a conflict.

Nine Degrees of Shadow

1. *Seraphim.* Also called the Flaming Ones, the Opposing Ones. *Opposing*, in this case, means opposite in nature or energy, not working against anything.

2. *Cherubim.* Also called the Hinderers and the Ophanim. This Degree of angels has the power to delay results until the timing is right.

3. *Thrones.* Also known as the Concealers and the Bene Elohim. Submission to patience; they conceal Mysteries and knowledge from those not ready to understand.

4. *Dominions.* Also called the Hashmallim and the Uncaring Ones. Dominions are considered to be dispassionate and indifferent to everything except the Supreme Power and balance. They are neutral in their working, and teach that there should be no extremes in thoughts or actions.

5. *Virtues.* Also known as the Deceivers, the Seducers, and the Malachim. The traditional names *Deceivers* and *Seducers* are misleading. These great angels work with ethics, and how to apply them to each life. Primarily, they teach us how not to deceive ourselves into believing something is right, when deep inside we know it isn't.

6. *Powers.* Also called the Ishim, the Illusioners, and the Separators. Here again, the traditional names can be mislead-

ing. This Degree of angels have the knowledge of spiritual truths. This has nothing to do with human-made churches and their laws, but with the higher laws. They also teach how to separate true psychic visions from the self-created ones.

7. *Nations (Principalities)*. The Gnostics called them the Archons. Also called the Elokim and the Agitators. Although associated with disorder, humiliation, and chaos, these angels work with the Multiversal laws, which ensure that for great changes to occur, things must be dismantled and reassembled in a different manner.

8. *Archangels*. Also called the Balancers, Angels of Darkness, the Princes, and the Watchers.

9. *Angels.* Also known as the Companions and the Guardians.

At the top of the two columns (again, refer to page 81 for the diagram), symbolized by the sphere numbered 11, are three higher areas leading to the Supreme Power. These are called (lowest to highest): the Forming Energy, the Thought Without Interest or Plan, and finally, the Limitless Shadow.

There is an invisible Gate that lies between the Dominions and the Thrones. This is numbered 10 on the illustration. Angel workers and Light-bringers can use this shortcut to go from one set of Degrees to the reverse ones. This gate is called the Abyss on the Light side and the Brilliant Height on the Shadow Side. In Jewish mysticism, the gate is known as Da'ath. It is ruled by Zagzagel (Divine Splendor), the Angel of Wisdom, a Prince of the Presence, a teacher of angels, and one who speaks all languages of the Multiverse. He is traditionally believed to guard the fourth level of Powers, but to reside in the seventh level of the Dominions. In other words, the angel is very powerful, extremely knowledgeable, and very little is known about him. He has the power to deny anyone passage through the invisible Gate between the Degrees of Light and Shadow.

Shadow Angels

Several illuminating manuscripts, written up to one hundred years before and after Jesus's supposed birth, were deliberately not included in what is today known as the orthodox Christian Bible. These texts are not even included in the Catholic Bible, which has extra chapters tucked in between the Old and New Testaments. All of these eliminated manuscripts are collectively called the apocryphal books. These contain some very interesting stories that shed new light on, and raise new questions about, certain biblical tales. Unfortunately, each new translator in ancient times added, subtracted, or changed the ideas and/or wording to fit the religio-political agenda of that period. It was not until recent new translations directly from original texts were released that we began to see a great many religious ideas in a new light, particularly the subject of "fallen" angels.

The apocryphal books that were originally written during Old Testament times offer us a very different insight into angels, the supposed Fall, and angelic interaction with humans than do the "accepted" Old Testament books. The true author or authors of these apocryphal texts are unknown, but obviously this material was the basis for the manuscripts that were later put into the New Testament Book of Revelation.

These apocryphal texts, especially the Books of Enoch, contain three stories of angels and their reactions to humans and each other that are not found elsewhere. One story tells how God created the human Adam and then demanded that all angels bow to this newly created being. Whether one takes this to be a literal or metaphorical command, it goes against Multiversal laws of worshiping one Supreme Power. The archangel Michael immediately bows to Adam, but his equal archangel (some say his twin brother) Lucifer refuses. The basis for the refusal is that all beings are created equal, and no such honor should be given to anyone or anything, except the Higher Power, or God.

Although the angels all knew this to be true, Lucifer and a number of other angels who refused were thrown out of heaven. Some translations of this story say the "fallen" angels were sent to earth, while others say the rebels were thrown into an eternal, tormenting hell.

Since Lucifer knew the law of not bowing to any except the Supreme Power, he was correct not to bow to humans. It appears as if "God" set up a no-win situation to separate Lucifer from the Light angels.

Nowhere does the Bible give more than sketchy details of the war between the angels. John the Apostle provides the most known facts. However, when John became a hermit, his writing went from reporting facts as he knew them to the very weird. He must have found psychedelic mushrooms or became a schizophrenic personality in his Revelation days.

The disagreement of bowing and breaking a spiritual law appears more along the line of the younger punk rockers annoying their elders and questioning "tradition." Rather like Lucifer saying to God, "Hey dude. Don't you think you could give humans and angels a break? You only seem to be happy when you've got your foot on somebody's neck. You know you have this problem of being completely neutral without emotions. Lighten up, will you? We're following the spiritual laws you gave us."

God/Goddess, who created everything, gave all beings free-will choice. It is reasonable, then, that highly intelligent angels have free will also. Angelic entities are of a much higher vibration than humans, and therefore more adherent to the desires of the Supreme Being than we usually are. Something has been left out of the story, something so crucial that it changed the human understanding of angels completely. My guess is that the Supreme Power, after lowering its energies to the point of duality for manifestation, deliberately created all angels to bridge the gap between Itself and the rest of Its creations. Since the angels are the first link in duality for the Creator, then it is reasonable that there should be one set of Light angels (positive energy) and one set of balancing Shadow angels (negative energy).

All angels are portrayed as having both positive and negative abilities and traits. For example, the archangel Michael is well-loved as a protector, yet he also directs certain destructive wars and events on earth. I'm sure that the angels who destroyed Sodom and Gomorrah didn't personally remove every child in those cities to avoid killing any innocents. I also know that angels are far less emotional than humans, but they do have a certain degree of emotions. They are not automatons, but living entities. As Multiversal law states that every creation contains both positive and negative, male and female. So even angels would have dual types of energy, some of them having more of one energy than another.

The second story, closely connected to the first one, doesn't mention Adam. It states that Lucifer and similarly thinking angels tried to take over heaven. A valid, solid reason for this coup is never given. The end result is that the archangel Michael and his cohorts waged terrible war on the archangel Lucifer and his followers, finally throwing them out of heaven. This tale makes no sense at all since nothing is more powerful than the Supreme Power, and that Power does not make mistakes.

Before any reader comes up with the "them against us" theory of modern religion, I will say here that there is a class of entities that are pure evil, but they are not angels. These beings are demons who choose to be basically pure evil. They are against every other being and entity in the Multiverse. However, demons are not the so-called "fallen" angels. All Light and Shadow angels are the counterbalance to the purely evil demons.

The third story comes from the Books of Enoch; these Books frequently contradict themselves from one section to another. So we will try to piece together a reasonable tale from the remaining ancient texts.

One must remember that, as with all religious stories, many of the events were colored by the cultural laws of that time and place. Because of their continuous fight for existence, the Jewish clans at that time had laws that forbade intermarriage with other cultures, as well as certain rules that "protected" women by giving their male relatives control over them.

In Enoch's reports, a group of angels called the Watchers was appointed to live on earth to monitor the progress of humans. The Book of the Watchers, a collection of writings found in the First Book of Enoch, specifically states that the Watchers were sent by God. They were not thrown out of heaven, but sent to earth!

There is no clear explanation of the duties of these Watchers. They weren't considered "fallen" or "evil" angels; they were on earth on a mission from the Otherworld. They were probably specially chosen, perhaps to add angelic blood or essence to the human gene pool, which was definitely struggling at that period in history. Although this story is recorded in Jewish history, there are hints in other cultures that similar events with angels occurred elsewhere, too. This interbreeding tells us an interesting fact: that some angels are able to produce offspring with other beings, although the majority of angels either cannot, or choose not to.

The Watchers were highly intelligent angels who fell in love with and married human women. The earthly Watchers were also called the Grigori (egoroi or egregori). Their offspring were generically called the Nephilim. These children were tall, very strong, brave, and intelligent.

The Watcher angels didn't force themselves on human women, seduce them, or merely live with them. They *married* them. This means that the angels met the marriage contract laws and ceremonies set down by each bride's father or the patriarch of her family. These laws and ceremonies were traditionally considered to have been given to humans (Jewish and otherwise) by a Higher Power. In that time period, the male members of a family chose the woman's husband, bargained on the dowry, and were very careful about who they added to their clan by marriage. These Watchers passed all the family tests and engaged in the honorable ceremony of legal marriage. Since all strangers were viewed with suspicion, we must assume that the Watchers also passed some form of spiritual tests before they were ever allowed to meet with the women.

Because these Watchers loved their wives, children, and the families into which they were accepted, they taught humans such knowledge as metallurgy, astrology, astronomy, geometry, mathematics, dancing, cosmetics, jewelry making, reading, and writing, among others. Undoubtedly, the women loved the jewelry, dancing, and cosmetics, all of which gave them more self-confidence. And the men likely appreciated the training in how to make swords and shields for defense, as well as how to plan strategy and use those weapons. These new abilities meant they had a better chance to defend their families and survive in a harsh world.

As with everything new, there had to be some traditionalists who decided all this new knowledge wasn't good. That the old ways were the only good ways. Therefore, some of the humans decided that the Watchers were up to no good. That probably didn't prevent the complainers from enjoying the newfound fruits of agriculture, herbal medicine, and building better houses.

Presided over by Salameil, the Watchers became known in Jewish and early Christian literature as the Unholy Ones, because these angels taught humans skills that were considered to be questionable or undesirable. However, I can't see how learning metallurgy, how to make jewelry, use astrology, or compound cosmetics is undesirable. But, for reasons unknown to us today, the knowledge brought by the Watchers was labeled as sinful. Regardless, most people, except for the fanatics, used this knowledge.

As religious literature often does, the recorders must have decided that the Watchers shouldn't be allowed to go down in history as loving, useful beings. So the recorders began writing down the "punishment" of the Watchers. The only problem was, few of them could agree on how that story went. There are several different versions within the Books of Enoch alone.

One tale says God condemned them all to die, and just killed them. A later version changed the end to death by drowning in the great flood of Noah. A third story, obviously written by someone into horrific punishments, says that the Watchers were thrown into a bottomless pit of fire and torture, with the entrance sealed forever by huge boulders.

First, the Supreme Power/God would not kill the Watchers, for they were following divine orders to do what they did. Second, being angels as well as Watchers, these beings were not vulnerable to an earthly death, such as drowning. And their descendants who were strong and very intelligent would not sit around watching Noah build a huge boat without asking why, and then building boats for their own families. Third, no earthly pit of fire, covered by boulders, would logically imprison angels, who have the ability to go to the Otherworld as they want. These "punishments and death" endings were obviously written by religious critics who wanted to kill any ideas among the people that the Supreme Power cared enough for its human creations that all of us were allowed to share a little angelic blood and learn some very vital knowledge to help us survive in a tough environment.

So through these fragmented pieces of religious history, we finally begin to see the reality and truth of the Shadow angels. They are as beautiful, loving, and helpful as any angels, and are the balance of the Light angels. This is in accordance with all Multiversal laws.

The following list of Shadow angels is by no means complete. I've deleted all the obvious names that were associated with the deities of other cultures, and therefore considered evil. I have also deleted all the false, contrived titles that refer to the devil. Shadow angels are not demons or evil, and demonic names and references have no place in this list of angels.

List of Shadow Angels

Abbadon: The Destroyer, the Dark Angel, Angel of Death and Destruction. Sometimes, he is equated with Sammael. Evil, discord, war, devastation. The extreme opposite of Light, but necessary to reveal and dismantle imbalanced energies so they can be reformed in a more usable form.

Adramelek: King of Fire. Also called Adramelech. Shown with a bearded human head, wings, and the body of a lion. Mischief, guile, ambition, malice, hypocrisy. Was known to the Babylonians and Assyrians.

Agares: Also called Agreas. He teaches all languages and has the ability to cause earthquakes.

Amezyarak: Also called Amazarec, Semyaza, and Amiziras. One of the earthly Watchers, who taught humans to cut and multiply roots; also taught the art of magick.

Araqiel: Also called Arakiel, Araquiel, Araciek, Arqel, Arkiel, Arkas, and Saraquael. One of the earthly Watchers; he taught humans to recognize the signs of good and bad crop times on earth.

Armaros: Also called Araros, Pharmaros, Abaros, and Arearos. One of the earthly Watchers. He taught humans how to break enchantments.

Asmoday: Also called Ashmedai, Ashmeday, Asmodius, and Sydoney. Belonging to the Virtues, he rules the powers of the moon under the name of Hasmoday. He taught humans mathematics, how to read the future, and the secrets of invisibility.

Asmodeus: Creature of Judgment, Raging Fiend. Also called Asmoday and Chammaday. Known to the Persians and Egyptians. He oversees all gambling houses. He taught humans music, dancing, drama, and how to create new fashions.

Astaroth: Also called Asteroth, Ashteroth, and Ashtoreth. Associated with dragons and snakes; also with the moon and the month of April. She was known to the Phoenicians and Syrians as Queen of Heaven. Belongs to the seraphim. Feminine personal power and beauty.

Azariel: Controls the waters on earth. He is also ruler of one of the twenty-eight mansions (days) of the moon. Helps with the use of moon magick.

Azazel: God Strengthens. Also called Azael and Hazazel. A member of the cherubim, he refused to bow to Adam. One of the earthly Watchers, he taught men the art of metallurgy and how to make swords and shields. He also taught women how to make and use cosmetics.

Barakiel: Lightning of God. Also called Baraqijal, Barakel, Baraqel, and Baraqiel. Element: East, Air, or Wind. Planet: Jupiter, the moon. Zodiac: Scorpio. He taught humans the art of astrology. One of the earthly Watchers, or the Grigori.

Barbatos: A great leader of the Virtues. One of the earthly Watchers, he taught humans how to understand the songs of birds, how to travel back in time to learn what happened in the past, and how to predict the future. He helps with magick only if the moon or sun is in the sign of Sagittarius.

Barbiel: An archangel and member of the Virtues. Also called Barbuel and Baruel. He is associated with February, October, and one of the twenty-eight days of the moon.

Belial: Prince of Darkness. Also called Beliar and Barial. An angel who is part of the Virtues, he is considered to be the ambassador to Turkey. He was created as a greater angel of vengeance than Michael.

Belphagor: Lord of Opening. Also called Belfagor. An angel of Nations, the ambassador to France and Paris. She teaches sexuality and its enjoyable uses beyond procreation. An earthly Watcher, she taught humans how to make important discoveries in all areas by asking questions and how to invent unique items.

Caim: Also called Caym and Camio. A member of the order of angels. He is good at settling disputes and giving answers about the future. He also teaches how to understand and predict through the voice of moving water.

Duma: Silence, Angel of the Stillness of Death. Also called Doumah and Dumath. Considered as the ambassador to Egypt, therefore he would be a member of Nations. Described as having a thousand eyes, armed with a flaming sword. Vindication.

Exael: An earthly Watcher who taught humans to work with silver and gold, and cut and set gems in jewelry.

Ezequeel: Strength of God. An earthly Watcher, he taught humans how to predict by watching the clouds.

Forcas: Also called Foras, Forras, Furcas, and Fourcas. A powerful angel of knowledge, he teaches mathematics, rhetoric, and logic. He can also teach magicians how to be inconspicuous or invisible, as well as how to find and restore lost objects.

Forneus: A member of the Thrones, he teaches art, rhetoric, and all languages. He also knows spells to make your enemies love you, or at least cease being enemies.

Gadreel: God is my Helper. Also called Gadriel. An earthly Watcher, this angel taught men the strategy of war and fighting abilities.

Hauras: Also called Flauros. Associated with leopards. He can give true answers about the past, present, and future.

Helayaseph: Also called Jiluyaseph and Hilujaseph. The head of a thousand angels who regulate the seasons and any unusual seasonal changes.

Hutriel: Rod of God. It is his responsibility, along with others, to punish nations that get out of hand and break laws.

Imamish: A member of Nations, he supervises voyages, their outcomes, and sailors. He also can destroy and humiliate enemies if asked.

Kafziel: Speed of God. Also sometimes called Cassiel. He helps rule over the planet Saturn, and governs the death of kings and rulers.

Kokabel: Star of God. Also called Kokabiel, Kochbiel, Kakabel, and Kabaiel. Tradition says he commands 365,000 angels and spirits. He knows all the secrets and lore of the stars, constellations, and astrology.

Kushiel: Rigid One of God. One of seven angels of retribution, she punishes nations with a whip of fire.

Kutiel: An angel who teaches the use of divining rods.

Lilith: Tradition says she was Adam's first wife, who left because she didn't like his controlling attitude or the fact that he took Eve as a second wife. She teaches sexual techniques, female independence, and sexual freedom for women.

Lucifer: Light Giver, Child of Light, Bearer of Light, and Morning Star. Leader of the Shadow angels and the earthly

Watchers. Chief of the Supreme Mysteries and the Recording Angels. Like the Light angel Michael, Lucifer was a prince of archangels and given more power than the seraphim. He was not associated with the leader of demons until Saint Jerome's dubious writings (ca. 347–420). Element: Storm or combination of all. Planets: Uranus, Neptune, Pluto, Chiron, Ceres, Pallas, Juno, and Vesta, as well as any retrograde planets. Incense: frankincense. Color: violet, purple, blackish-gray.

Marchosias: Also called Marbas and Marchocias. He knows about secret or hidden things; he has the knowledge that cures diseases. His specialty, however, is the teaching of mechanical arts.

Mastema: The Accusing Angel, Angel of the Lord, Angel of Hostility. Also called Mansemat and Mastemah. Adversity, destruction, justice.

Naamah: Pleasing. Traditionally called one of the four angels of prostitution, along with Lilith, Eisheth, and Agrat bat Mahlat. What this means is that she is another female angel who upholds the independence and freedom for women.

Nelchael: Belongs to the Degree called Thrones. He teaches astronomy, geography, and mathematics.

Penemue: The Inside. Also called Tamal, Tamuel, and Tumael. Invoke Penemue in magick against stupidity. He taught humans to differentiate between bitter and sweet tastes. This earthly Watcher also taught them to make paper and ink, to use an alphabet, to write, and to read. He knows much secret wisdom.

Rahab: Violence, Prince of the Primordial Sea, Angel of Insolence and Pride. He rescued the Jewish *Sefer Raziel* that contains all knowledge and mystical secrets, after other angels threw it into the sea to prevent humans from using it. Call upon him for help with anything to do with the seas and oceans.

Ramiel: Also called Rumael, Remiel, Phanuel, and Yerahmeel. Ramiel presides over visions and judgment of sins.

Raum: Also called Raym; he belongs to the Degree of Thrones. He can predict the past, present, and future. He makes friends out of enemies. He can also destroy cities by presenting their government leaders opportunities to subvert their laws.

Rimmon: Exalted, the Roarer. An archangel known to Syria and Babylon; called the ambassador to Russia. He has power over storms, lightning, and thunder.

Salamiel: Prince of the Grigori and Watchers.

Sammael: Angel of Death, Severity of God. Also called Samael, Samil, Salmael, and Seir. One of the greatest archangelic magicians, and at one time higher than the seraphim. The ruler of Mars, he can create or destroy temptation.

Sariel: Also called Sarkiel, Saraqael, Sarqel, and Zerachiel. He rules the zodiac sign Aries, is one of the nine angels of the summer solstice, and teaches about the courses of the moon and their effects.

Semyaza: Strength. Also called Semiaza, Shemeyza, Semjaza, and Shemhazai. He is a member of the seraphim and an earthly Watcher. Victory, happiness. Agriculture, root cuttings, enchantments.

Shaftiel: Lord of the Shadow of Death. He punishes earthly nations who are aggressive against other nations because of differences in beliefs and ideals.

Shamshiel: Light of Day, Mighty Sun of God, Prince of Earthly Paradise. Also called Shamsiel. A Watcher, who teaches astrology and spell-binding power. Also teaches the powers of the signs (zodiac signs) of the sun.

Temeluch: Merciless Angel, All Fire. Also called Temeluchus, Temleyakos, Abtelmoluchos, and Tataruchus. She is the caretaker and protector of children at birth and during infancy.

Turel: Rock of God. Also called Turael. He knows the powers of the planet Jupiter.

Uzziel: Strength of God. Also called Usiel. He is a member of the cherubim, Virtues, and Malakim. One of the nine angels who control the four winds.

Vapula: He appears as a lion with griffin wings. He teaches skill in handicrafts, philosophy, and all sciences contained in books.

Vassago: A Prince of the Shadow angels. He can predict past, present, and future events. He will help find anything that is lost or hidden. He can also uncover a woman's deepest secrets.

Vual: Also called Uvall and Voval. He is a member of the Ischim, or Powers. He is an angel of predictions and can make enemies become friends. When invoked in spells, he can help win the love of women.

Xaphan: Also called Zephon. An angel who became dissatisfied with the way he was treated and overlooked for missions, he set fire to heaven and got kicked out. (I just couldn't resist including this angel.)

Zagan: He can appear as a bull with griffin wings. He has the
power to make humans clever and witty, and can make any
fool wise. He also knows how to turn any metal into money.
He can turn any water into wine, blood, or oil.

Working with Shadow Angels

As I mentioned in the chapter on Light angels, each archangel has an astral temple that exists in the astral plane. These
are found above earthly sacred spots. This applies whether the
temples belong to Light angels or Shadow angels. The Shadow
angels also have a huge Shadow chamber where they can all
meet as they wish.

*(Use the cleansing method mentioned on page 16, and the medi-
tation beginning practices listed on page 23.)*

Your guardian angels are at your side, reassuring you
that you will never be in any danger or difficulty during
this meditation. Quickly, you and your guardians move
through the misty veil that separates the earth plane from
the astral plane. A magnificent crystal half-sphere hangs
in the heavens ahead of you. Thousands of angels are
entering this temple.

As you enter this dome, you discover that it is very
difficult to see much difference between the huge crowd
of Shadow angels and the Light angels you saw during a
previous meditation. The arrays of moving colors are just
as rich, the celestial music just as wonderful.

For a moment, you stand still, listening intently to the
sunrise song of the Light angels blending perfectly with
the sunset song of the Shadow angels. This constant song,
which blends with the music of the planets, has always

existed. You realize now that anytime you become quiet, you can hear and feel the balance this music produces in everything throughout the Multiverse. It has always been there for you. You simply hadn't known to listen for it before.

Your personal guardian angels appear before you, smiling as you discover there is no evil in the Shadow angel chamber, merely another type of creating energy.

"I am your guardian Light angel," one of the beings tells you.

"And I am your guardian Shadow angel," the other says. "We work in pairs so that you are always surrounded by a balance of energy. You sometimes feel out of balance simply because you do not recognize the companionship of one of us."

They walk with you through the angelic crowds so you can see the light shows of energy and colors that are reflected by different areas of walls of the great dome. Some of the patterns produce scenes of sacred spots around the earth.

You notice other humans with their guardian angels, experiencing the Shadow angel chamber for the first time, just as you are. If you wish, you may talk to these humans. Your guardian angels also introduce you to a few Shadow angels whose powers match the goals you are working toward. Except for feeling the mighty power and intelligence of these great celestial beings, you recognize only their love and desire to help radiating from them.

When you have seen enough for this visit, your guardians assure you that you may return at any time. They tell you that it may take you some time to assimilate all you have seen and learned.

Quickly, but gently, your guardians return you to your physical body.

(End of meditation)

Chants and Petitions

Whether you petition the Shadow angels within a cast circle, burn candles and papers, or merely speak to them in a private talk, you may wish to coordinate candle colors to the type of request you are asking. See page 104 for a list of colors and their meanings.

If you want to place stones on your altar for the Shadow angels, magicians traditionally use black obsidian, tektites, smoky quartz, and labradorite. However, as with any angel ritual, quartz crystal works just fine.

The recipe for making holy water to sprinkle on your altar or around in your house is given on page 33. Page 105 explains how to make a Light-angel oil to rub on your candles for attracting the powers of those angels. Following is how you make Shadow angel oil, so you'll be able to rub that on candles dedicated to those angels.

Shadow Angel Oil

Use a dark-colored bottle with a tight lid. Add one-half teaspoon pure almond oil to the bottle. Using an eyedropper, add one drop each of these oils: sandalwood, myrrh, patchouli, frankincense, and juniper. You may substitute cedar oil for juniper if you have difficulty finding that oil. Cap the bottle, and swirl very gently to mix. Rub on the appropriate candle when doing candle burning and other Shadow angel rituals. Store the bottle in a dark, cool place. Sunlight will evaporate the essential oils or change their scents.

Shadow Angel Chant

Goddess Version

(You may rub Shadow angel oil on a gray candle to burn during this chant. Or you may rub the oil on a candle that represents a goal you wish these angels to help you with. If you want, you may talk to the Shadow angels, using your own words instead of this chant. You may also write out a request in one of the angelic alphabets and burn the paper in a metal bowl at the end of your chant.)

> *Shadow is needed to see the Light*
> *Just as day must have the night.*
> *Blending both gives me the power*
> *To manifest my goals in any hour.*
> *I acknowledge the truth in Shadow and Light*
> *A balance of Multiversal might.*
> *I ask the angels of each Degree*
> *To fulfill my wish. So mote it be.*

Pagan Version

(You may rub Shadow angel oil on a gray or black candle that is placed on the left side of your altar, and the Light angel oil on a white candle placed on the right side of the altar. Or you may rub both oils on a candle that represents a goal you wish the angels to help you with. In this case, rub both oils from the wick of the candle toward the bottom.)

You may wish to include this chant with a regular cast circle, as described in the appendix. If you cast a circle, it is best to call up the four archangels for the four directions.

If you desire, write out your request in one of the angelic alphabets and burn the paper in a metal bowl at the end of the ritual, just before closing the circle.

Cast your circle and call upon the four directional guardians. Then face your altar.

Angels of Shadow, we bid you welcome and thank you for your presence. (Light the gray or black candle.)

Angels of Light, we bid you welcome and thank you for your presence. (Light the white candle.)

Balance of energies is the key of life
Of manifestation and spiritual enlightenment.
Nothing of evil or imbalance shall exist here.
Only balance and goodness that is Goddess-sent.

(Turn the palm of your left hand toward the Shadow angel candle and the palm of your right hand toward the Light angel candle, while deeply breathing in the combined energy.)

My body, mind, and spirit are renewed
Through the power of the breaths I take.
I am now balanced as I was meant to be.
My sleeping spiritual self will now awake.

(*You may now do a short meditation, or burn your request paper if you made one. Then close your circle.*)

New Age Version

(*You may rub Shadow angel oil on a gray candle to burn during this chant. Or you may rub the oil on a candle that represents a goal you wish these angels to help you with. If you so choose, you may talk to the Shadow angels using your own words instead of this chant. You may also write out a request in one of the angelic alphabets and burn the paper in a metal bowl at the end of your chant.*)

Both columns of angels that rise above
Were created to bring us eternal love.
Their powers entwined can conquer all
Answering my needs when I do call.
Shadow and Light, raise me spiritually.
As I do wish, so shall it be.

7. HIGHER-LEVEL RITUALS

Combined Angels Rituals

Obviously, working with both the Light and Shadow angels together isn't a magick to play with. It is serious business. If you choose not to work with Shadow angels, or if you choose to do a combination of angels ritual, that is fine. There are enough suggestions in this book about working with Light angels, guides, and guardians to make your reading worthwhile. Never involve yourself in magick of which you are afraid. Fear puts a broom handle in the magickal spokes of spells and rituals. You may be able to work past your fear programming later. If not, that's okay, too. But at least acquaint yourself with the true history of the Shadow angels and consider the possibilities.

Think of science's discoveries of different types of light, from ordinary everyday light through the spectrum to black light and ultraviolet, into realms that we can't see. Then you can better understand that Lucifer's "light" is a perfect balance for that of Michael. Successful magick results from strong intent and creating a balance of positive and negative energy (light). Everything that exists, or is brought into existence through magick and prayer, contains a mixture of both energies (lights).

If you wish to represent both Light and Shadow angels by candles on your altar, use a gray for the Shadow angels on the left of your altar and a white for the Light angels on the right side. If you can't find a gray candle, which can often be difficult to do, you can use black. By using both candles, you can call upon a balance of negative and positive angelic energies.

Have four small quartz crystals on the altar, along with your written request and a metal bowl to burn it in. Frankincense and/or myrrh incense are always attracting to angels and all good spirits.

As an example for a combined ritual, we will call upon the Light angel Gabriel for new beginnings and psychic powers along with the Shadow angel Semyaza for victory, happiness, and enchantments. By using two angels with the same powers, but different energies, we can amplify the ability raised within the circle to manifest our goals. Just make certain the goal you have written down fits into the categorical powers of these angels.

Use the cleansing method mentioned on page 16 before beginning the combined ritual.

Cast your circle, using the directions given in the appendix. Call upon the four archangels that represent the four directions.

Return to face your altar. Turn the palm of your left hand toward the Shadow angel candle and the palm of your right hand toward the Light angel candle, while deeply breathing in the combined energy. Say:

My body, mind, and spirit are renewed
Through the power of the breaths I take.
I am now balanced as I was meant to be.
My sleeping spiritual self will now awake.

Keep your left palm toward the gray candle while saying:

Shadow angels, welcome here.
Let me feel your presence clear.
Blend your powers with those of Light
That my goal may manifest just right.

Turn the palm of your right hand toward the white candle, saying:

Angels of Light, all Degrees of Nine
Let me feel your presence divine.
Link with the Shadow Ones, brethren of power
That my desire be created in this hour.

Take the small quartz crystals in one hand and your written request in your power hand. Moving clockwise, go to the east. Lay one of the crystals inside the circle in that direction. Hold up your request, and say:

> *All angels of the powers of Air*
> *Here is my request. Please make it clear.*

Moving clockwise, go to the south. Lay one of the crystals inside the circle in that direction. Hold up your request, and say:

> *All angels of the powers of Fire*
> *Pour your energies into my desire.*

Moving clockwise, go to the west. Lay one of the crystals inside the circle in that direction. Hold up your request, and say:

> *All angels of the powers of Water*
> *Fulfill this goal and no other.*

Moving clockwise, go to the north. Lay one of the crystals inside the circle in that direction. Hold up your request, and say:

> *All angels of the powers of Earth*
> *Aid me to bring this goal to birth.*

Return to the altar. Fold your request paper in half, and then in half again. Quickly, light one corner of the paper from the gray candle and another corner from the white candle. Drop the paper in the metal bowl to burn it. As it burns, concentrate on holding a mental image of your desire in a completed state.

Again, turn your left palm toward the gray candle and your right palm toward the white candle. Say:

> *I call Earth to bind my spell. Air to speed its travel well.*
> *Bright as Fire shall it glow. Deep as tide of Water flow.*
> *Count the elements fourfold, and in the fifth the spell shall hold.*
> *Shadow angels and Light, I thank you all*
> *For answering my magickal call.*

You may now do a short meditation if you wish. Or you may close the circle, as described in the appendix.

This combined ritual can be used with any pair of Shadow and Light angels who complement each other in powers.

8. Appendix

Chakras

The word *chakra* comes from the ancient Sanskrit language of India. It means "wheel of light or fire." The chakras are not found in the actual physical body, but in the closest aura layer to the body. These invisible whirling access points create a connection between the human body and Multiversal energy. Humans are more than just physical bodies. We are a physical body with multiple, surrounding bodies of varying rates of energy vibrations. Just as the physical body needs food and water to exist, so the other bodies need nourishment of *prana*, or spiritual energy. The chakras draw the necessary prana from the Multiverse, through all the aura layers and into the human body.

Although there are hundreds of chakras, most of them considered to be minor, I have listed nine major chakras and two sets of minor chakras on the chart on the next page. Westernized teachings usually mention the first seven chakras that directly affect certain body parts and endocrine glands.

Although there are dozens of what are called *minor chakras* in the body, you really need only be concerned at this time about two pairs and a single minor chakra. The first set of minor chakras that you use daily without thinking about them are found in the palm of each hand. They are capable of both drawing in, and sending out, streams of Multiversal energy. The predominant hand (the one you use for writing) is the most powerful for channeling this energy into yourself or another, while the other hand draws off and gets rid of unwanted or negative energy.

The second set of minor chakras are found in the sole of each foot. They are actually connected to what some people call the *Earth Star*, a powerful Earth connection just between and below the feet. This pair of chakras keeps us balanced by siphoning off excess energy or grounding us physically with a good dose of Earth energy.

The first major chakra is the base, or root, chakra found at the very end of the spinal column; it is red. This is your survival center that corresponds to physical needs, willpower, and either success or failure in your life. The sacral, also called the spleen or belly chakra, lies just below the navel in the center of the abdomen; it is orange. It corresponds to the lower emotional aspects of life, sexuality, procreation, and personal

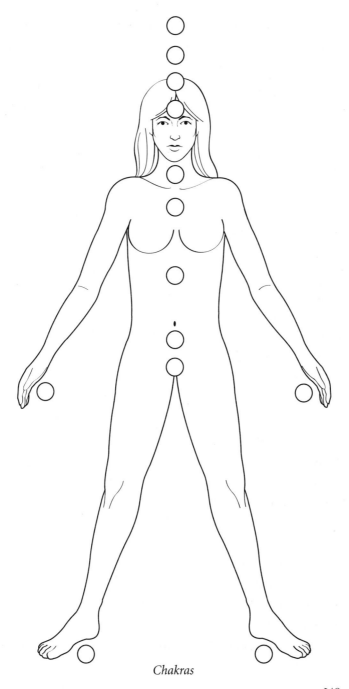

Chakras

pleasures. The solar plexus chakra is yellow and is centered just above the navel in the middle of the abdomen. Often referred to as the body's second brain, this chakra represents the lower mental aspects. It is the source meant when one speaks of intuition, "feeling" something, or a gut feeling. These three lower chakras are primarily connected with the Earth, its energies, and the physical body.

The green heart chakra lies in the center of the upper chest, the seat of compassion and love in their truest definitions. The throat chakra, a true blue or turquoise, is found in the front area of the throat, just above the points of the collarbone. This is the center for communication on any level, plus the creativity connected with the verbal or nonverbal voice (the strong mental thoughts). These two chakras are the intermediary and bridging points between the physical and spiritual ones.

Nearly everyone knows that the brow chakra is also called the psychic third eye. This purplish-blue chakra is in the middle of the forehead, just above the eyebrows, and enables each person to develop and experience psychic abilities. The last of the seven major "body" chakras is the crown at the top of the head; it is violet. This center, when open and unblocked, enables a person to grow spiritually in whatever path he or she chooses. These are the last major chakras directly connected with the physical body.

The eighth, or transpersonal, chakra lies about eighteen inches above the crown chakra. It isn't directly connected with the physical body or any endocrine glands. It shows as either a pure white or a flashing of rainbow colors. The energy here is transitional—that is, beyond the ego or personal self. As a transitional center, it links the physical and spiritual areas of each person.

The ninth, or universal (or Multiversal), chakra is about six inches above the transpersonal chakra. It is completely disconnected from any attachment to the personal level. It has no links with anything physical, but is a direct pipeline to the Goddess/the God/the Supreme Creative Force. This is a very difficult chakra to see, as it shimmers in gold and silver at a very high vibration.

When working with your guides, guardians, and angels, your heart and throat chakras will likely be the first to be strongly activated. As you work with meditation and spiritual communication, slowly raising your vibrations, the sixth through the ninth chakras will begin to clear and come into importance. The heart chakra bridges the upper and lower body chakras, as the crown creates a bridge to the higher chakras. Humans need to raise their general vibrational rate of the higher chakras in order to establish and clean communications with the Otherworld.

One other minor chakra that I consider important to these studies is the one found at the center of the back of the neck, at the base of the skull. This chakra makes a unique two-way connection with two upper chakras and their endocrine glands, besides its direct influence on the part of the brain known as the medulla oblongata. The energy taken in by this chakra is channeled up through the medulla oblongata, from which it branches in two directions. This energy continues on to the pituitary gland and the brow chakra, as well as to the pineal gland and the crown chakra. When this connecting passageway is unblocked and developed, even for short periods of time, you become very aware of your spirit helpers and other astral beings.

Auras

Although we usually speak as though each person has one aura, we all actually have several layers of auras. Each layer extends farther from the physical body than the layer before it. Writers differ on the number of aura layers, as they do the number of chakras. I believe that, at this point in our development, we can only access and influence eleven layers of the aura, and therefore I will only discuss those.

The first five aura layers are concerned with, and connected to, the five lower chakras, as well as being influenced by what the person thinks, feels, and is experiencing in his or her daily life.

The sixth aura layer links with the brow chakra in the center of the forehead. It helps with cross-time travel, Otherworld journeys, finding parallel universes, and expanding the use of psychic abilities.

The seventh layer links each person with their past, present, and future. It corresponds to the crown chakra. If a past life or lives are directly influencing and affecting the present life, evidence of that will be found in this layer.

The eighth layer looks like an iridescent egg shape around the human body, often as thick as four feet. It has energy waves rippling through it at all times, as it contains evidence of all our personal experiences. This has earned it the name of the "tattle-tale" aura. It is connected with the transpersonal chakra above the head. If one's personal behavior is more to blame than outside influences for one's success, or lack thereof, it will show up in this aura.

The ninth layer (sometimes called the kethic aura) is the only auric layer that doesn't surround the body. It appears as a small, whirling, flat vortex, spinning above the head. Its objec-

Layers of Auras

tive is to connect all the aura layers with spiritual energy and the Otherworld. It is the body-place that contains the contents of a person's soul, or at least the door to that soul.

The tenth aura is also called the integrative layer. It is merely a pathway between the physical world and the Otherworld. Its stage of development determines how difficult the person finds it to astral travel.

The transmutational layer, or eleventh aura, sees that the complete person on all levels of existence is constantly nourished with a balanced energy flow from the very depths of the Earth and the very heights of the Multiverse.

The Otherworld Layout

The Otherworld is usually described as being of three levels: the Upperworld (a high spiritual plane), the Middleworld (a kind of alternative time-space to the earth plane), and the Lowerworld (a place of ancestors and the darker energy deities). The Lowerworld is not an evil place, nor a prison for evil entities.

See the map on page 156 for the entire layout of the Otherworld and its attendant side areas. By reviewing this layout, and reading about each level, a traveler can determine where he or she is when journeying.

During my years of journeying to the Otherworld, I became aware of two other levels, existent but not well-known. These are the Highest and the Underworld.

The Highest, which is above, but attached to the Upperworld, isn't visited by any beings except angels and archangels. I learned from the archangels that their specific areas are actually above the Highest. The Nine Degrees of Light and the Nine Degrees of Shadow rise about the Highest, until they reach the three outer veils that cloak the essence of the Supreme Creative Force. In the

Jewish system of the Kabalah, these veils are called the Ain, the Ain Soph, and the Ain Soph Aur.

Although travelers can't visit the Highest, they can go to the Golden Gate that separates it from the Upperworld. There, one can talk with the Goddess, the God, and the oldest mystical dragon (She Who Sleeps). It is also a meeting place for humans and angels.

The Upperworld is a level of great beauty and wisdom. Here are all the cultural deities ever worshiped on our world and on any other world in the Multiverse.

The Garden of Wisdom and Solitude, as well as healing gardens, are encased by high hedges, and are endless gardens of all cultures. They have a multitude of shrines, temples, gazebos, and flower-covered shelters. Flower-lined stone paths lead to small streams, waterfalls, fountains, and little bridges of ponds of golden fish.

The Middleworld is a fantastic level that is the dwelling place for elves, fairies, dragons, unicorns, other mythological creatures, and most spirit guides. Animal allies (power animals) are sometimes found here. However, the most likely place to meet power animals is in the Lowerworld.

The Akashic Record Keepers live in a small side area reached from the Middleworld. This area is called Akasha and works closely with the area Astra-Keepers, entered through a connection in the Upperworld. The Akashic Record Keepers keep all the Akashic Records for each being up-to-date, and they advise the judges in the Lowerworld Hall of Justice (the Council) who oversee the reincarnation process. If you visit the Hall of Akashic Records, you will find assistants ready to find your personal records and help you to understand them.

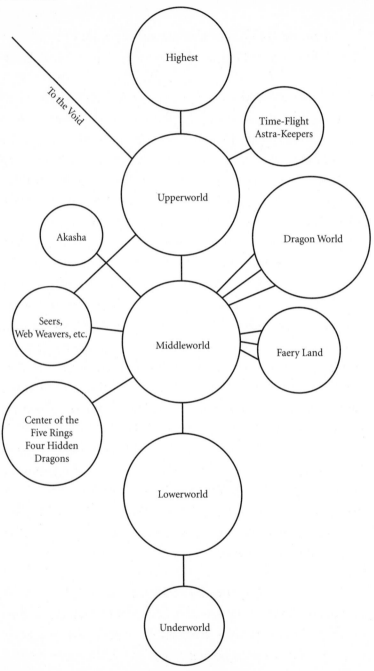

Map of the Otherworld

There are Gardens of Healing and Temples of Healing in the Middleworld that are similar to those found in the Upperworld.

The Lowerworld is a level of heavier vibrations, but it isn't a place of evil. Souls of your ancestors are found here. It is possible to meet very ancient ancestors and get a wondrous sense of continuity of your family's lines. All incoming and outgoing souls come here to the Council before they are allowed to reincarnate back into the physical world. Their natal charts and karmic debts are discussed with their spirit guides.

Travelers should never try to enter the Underworld. In fact, it is virtually impossible to do so, without a heavy guard of warrior dragons. This is for their maximum protection, since the Underworld *is* a prison for all the truly evil entities of the Multiverse. The Prison Gate on this level leads only into the Underworld, and confines these souls that are captured by warrior dragons and archangels. The only victims of the Underworld are each other. None of these souls can be refused the right to reincarnate, but most of them don't choose to, because of the awful, heavy karmic debt.

The map of the Otherworld and its subsidiary areas, as I know them, will help you identify where you are and what you may see during meditations. It could also be of use if you decide you want to visit one of the main levels. Just remember: you can't visit the Highest or the angelic realms, and it is safest to avoid the Underworld.

Casting a Ritual Circle

Learning to cast a magickal ritual circle isn't a necessary part of contacting your guides, teachers, guardians, or angels. Such a circle is for working greater magick with the help of these supporters. A circle contains the magickal energy you raise, and lets it build to a greater intensity until you focus totally on your goal and release the power that will affect that goal. This kind of circle has been used successfully for centuries by the magicians of many cultures. Today, such a sacred space is usually a standard part of rituals by those in Witchcraft and ceremonial magick.

The basic steps used to create this space are the same, although the wording may differ from person to person. First, the invisible circle line is drawn, followed by the calling up of the quarters, guardians, or directions.

The central part of the ceremony is the working of magick to obtain a goal, protect and defend yourself, do a healing, or work with deities with whom you are not quite comfortable. It can also provide an especially sealed area for very deep meditations, if you are uncomfortable about going into the Otherworld. Personally, I have never found that a circle was needed for meditation. However, if it makes you feel better, cast one. You focus completely, and without wavering, on the objective you want to attain, release the built-up magickal energy, and then chant a closing that seals the energy to your objective.

To end the ceremony, you dismiss the spiritual entities you called to guard and guide you in the beginning. Then, you "cut" the invisible circle with a downward swoop of your hand to dissipate it. This last movement grounds all remaining energy into the earth. Sometimes, I place my power hand on the floor for further grounding, if I feel that doing so is necessary.

If for any reason the circle is accidentally broken by a person crossing the invisible line, you should immediately dismiss the four watchers or guardians and direct all energy into the ground. If you don't do this, you will have random, undirected balls of magick drifting about, causing all kinds of disruptions. The only exception I have found to something or someone crossing and not disturbing the circle is a cat. Cats seem to have the ability to move into and out of a circle without breaking it or making an opening in the perimeter.

A circle casting can be as simple or as elaborate as you wish. You might feel more powerful if you wear special clothing or jewelry. You may not want to go through the blessing of salt and water, sprinkling the circle perimeter, or lighting candles at each direction. Nor do you need to have ritual tools. You don't even need candles or incense, although, to me, the tools, candles, and incense add to the atmosphere that builds the magick.

The absolutes you must do when performing circle magick are drawing the invisible line, calling up the directions, doing your work, dismissing the directions, and ritually cutting the circle. And of course you should have a small table in the center to use as an altar.

Rather than write about the ways different spiritual paths do things and why, I will simply give you several examples of each step so you can choose what feels best to you. Please do not mix the types of guardians for the directions. For example, don't call up a god, an angel, an animal, and something else, all at the same time for the directions. As you will see from the following examples, you should keep some continuity to the groups you use as guardians or watchers.

The circle-drawing always begins on the east side of your area and ends by overlapping the invisible ends in the east. Some magicians prefer to stand facing the east after the circle is cast and they begin their work. I believe this may have originated because the sun rises in the east. Others choose to stand facing the north while working; north is associated with the Earth element. I've always faced north when working alone, or stood in the north position when working with a partner. Things merely seemed to work better for me this way. I don't know of any rituals where the magician faced the west.

The position of your altar table is also not rigid. Some practitioners place their altar in the east, very close to the edge of the circle, while others put it in the north. I prefer my altar in the center so I can move all around it if necessary.

Whichever area you choose to cast your circle in, make certain it allows you at least enough room to move around and has a door that you can shut for privacy. It is amazing how casting a circle seems to attract people and critters who otherwise wouldn't be the least bit interested in what you do.

Each compass direction is traditionally associated with elements and colors. However, depending upon the culture, the colors may be different. If you decide to use the properly colored candle (according to the color group you choose), place the appropriate candle in a fireproof holder at the inner edge of the circle at the proper direction. You may put a white candle on the altar. You can use the white candle to light each direction candle in turn, or you can carry the white candle clockwise around the circle as you call up each direction. If you decide not to use candles, salute each direction with your raised palm as you call.

If you plan to do a candle spell that calls for a candle to burn out, set the holder inside a metal cauldron or bowl to guard against accidental fire. Votive candles can be used easily in a metal cauldron without a holder. Just put a thin layer of scented oil in the bottom of the cauldron; this will let you remove any remaining wax with little trouble. Just check that the scented oil matches the type of candle spell you are doing.

And, no, you don't have to do a ritual by candlelight only. It makes a great atmosphere if you use only candlelight, but it is also nearly impossible to read anything if you have written out your directions and spells. If you have to lean close to a candle to read, you may find yourself with a burning paper in your hand. Try to have a lamp bright enough to see by but not glaring. Dimmer switches and three-way lamps are great for ritual work.

Directional Colors

The four compass directions are coordinated with the four main elements, or building blocks, of magick. The names of the elemental beings associated with each direction differ from culture to culture, as do the colors. The European magickal tradition says that east is Air and mental processes; the south, Fire and action; the west, Water and emotions; and the north, Earth and material, physical things.

The Celtic tribes associated the east with red and dawn, the south with white and noon, the west with gray and twilight, and the north with black and midnight. They called the directions "castles of the four winds."

Qabalistic magicians associated the east with archangel Raphael and red, the south with archangel Michael and white, the west with archangel Gabriel and green, and the north with archangel Uriel and black.

In ancient China, they wrote of the Black Warrior, associated with the north, water, and black; the White Tiger, associated with the west, metal, and white; the Vermillion Bird, associated with the south, fire, red; and the Azure Dragon, associated with the east and green. They also mentioned the Four Hidden Dragons of Wisdom, but gave no colors.

The ancient Mayans associated east and red, south and yellow, west and black, and north and white. Other cultures in what is now Mexico used different colors. The Native American traditions used a variety of colors, depending upon the tribe.

Casting the Circle

Use the forefinger of your power hand (usually the one with which you write) or your ritual dagger. Begin in the east and visualize blue-white flames drawing a circle as you move clockwise around the area, overlapping and ending in the east.

Add a pinch of salt to a small cup of water. Hold your power hand over the cup, and say: *I bless you in the name of positive power.*

Lightly sprinkle the water clockwise around the circle, beginning and ending in the east.

Calling the Four Directions

If you use candles, light each one as you chant the welcome. If not, hold up your palm in salute. Begin in the east and move clockwise around the circle as you greet each guardian.

Archangels:

In the east, say: *I call upon you, Raphael, to protect and guide me.*

In the south, say: *I call upon you, Michael, to protect and guide me.*

In the west, say: *I call upon you, Gabriel, to protect and guide me.*

In the north, say: *I call upon you, Uriel, to protect and guide me.*

Lords and Ladies:
This can be used as a general call for deities or elementals.

Come, you Lords and Ladies of the east. I call upon you to help and protect me in this time of magick.

Come, you Lords and Ladies of the south. I call upon you to help and protect me in this time of magick.

Come, you Lords and Ladies of the west. I call upon you to help and protect me in this time of magick.

Come, you Lords and Ladies of the north. I call upon you to help and protect me in this time of magick.

Animal Allies or Power Animals:
If you have personal power animals that you want to include, change the names. However, be certain their traits match the direction.

North: Bear for stamina, revenge, transformation, dreams. Owl for silent movement, unmasking deceivers, finding hidden truths. Raven for messages from spirit, transformation, revealing paths to ancient Mysteries. Wolf for intelligence, outwitting enemies, dreams, intuition.

East: Elephant for confidence, patience, removal of obstacles. Horse for endurance, freedom, Otherworld travels, overcoming obstacles. Hummingbird for happiness, joy, relaxation, connection with nature spirits. Falcon for astral travel, soul healing, revealing hidden paths to knowledge.

South: Cobra has the ancient keys to the Mysteries, and brings very strict and strong teachers of great knowledge. Eagle for wisdom, long life, strength, courage, hidden spiritual truths. Rainbow-colored rattlesnake for great magickal power and the key to many Mysteries. Leopard for cunning, stealth, boldness, confidence.

West: Crow for prophecy, cunning skills, knowledge, secret wisdom, and connections to ancient deities. Dolphin for freedom, joy in life, ancient secrets of lost civilizations, releasing negative emotions. Dragonfly for dreams, mystical messages, visions of coming changes. Pegasus for inspiration and empowering the psychic on all levels.

Go to the east, and say: *Behold, you mighty falcon, power animal of Air. I do summon, stir, and call you up to witness this rite and to guard this circle.*

Go to the south, and say: *Behold, you mighty leopard, power animal of Fire. I do summon, stir, and call you up to witness this rite and to guard this circle.*

Go to the west, and say: *Behold, you mighty dolphin, power animal of Water. I do summon, stir, and call you up to witness this rite and to guard this circle.*

Go to the north, and say: *Behold, you mighty wolf, power animal of Earth. I do summon, stir, and call you up to witness this rite and to guard this circle.*

Dragons:
From Sairys (Sair-iss), *ruler of the eastern dragons fair, comes now the wondrous power of Air.*

From Fafnir (Faf'-near), *ruler of the dragons of the south, comes cleansing Fire from dragon mouth.*

From Naelyan (Nail'-yon), *ruler of dragons of the west, comes the power of Water, three times blessed.*

From Grael (Grail), *ruler of dragons of the north, the power of Earth does now come forth.*

Now is the time for you to do whatever magick you had planned: candle spells, writing out desires on paper and burning the paper, making talisman bags, or simply talking to those entities you called to join you. When you have finished with your work, you need to bind the spell to do its job. Stand facing your altar, your arms raised, and chant:

Spell Binding Chant:

I call Earth to bind my spell, Air to speed its travel well. Bright as Fire shall it glow. Deep as tide of Water flow. Count the elements fourfold, and in the fifth the spell shall hold. So mote it be!

Now you need to thank and dismiss your guardians, beginning in the east and moving clockwise around the circle.

Archangels:

East: *Farewell, Raphael. My thanks and blessings.*
South: *Farewell, Michael. My thanks and blessings.*
West: *Farewell, Gabriel. My thanks and blessings.*
North: *Farewell, Uriel. My thanks and blessings.*

Lords and Ladies:

East: *Go in peace, Lords and Ladies of the East. My thanks and blessings.*

South: *Go in peace, Lords and Ladies of the South. My thanks and blessings.*

West: *Go in peace, Lords and Ladies of the West. My thanks and blessings.*

North: *Go in peace, Lords and Ladies of the North. My thanks and blessings.*

Animal Allies or Power Animals:

Dismiss the power animals according to the one you chose for each direction.

East: *Depart in peace, powerful falcon of Air. I give my thanks and say fare you well.*

South: *Depart in peace, powerful leopard of Fire. I give my thanks and say fare you well.*

West: *Depart in peace, powerful dolphin of Water. I give my thanks and say fare you well.*

North: *Depart in peace, powerful wolf of Earth. I give my thanks and say fare you well.*

Dragons

East: *Go in peace, dragons of the East, and return again in the ritual hour.*

South: *Go in peace, dragons of the South, and return again in the ritual hour.*

West: *Go in peace, dragons of the West, and return again in the ritual hour.*

North: *Go in peace, dragons of the North, and return again in the ritual hour.*

Farewell to you, O dragons fair
Fire, Water, Earth, and Air.
Together we make magick well
By power deep and dragon spell.
In peace go now. Return once more
To teach me magick and ancient lore.
Draconis! Draconis! Draconis!

Closing the Circle:

Using the forefinger of your power hand or your ritual dagger, go to the east and "cut" down through the invisible circle. Say:

This circle is open but spiritually unbroken. The powers raised here go forth to create my desire. I give my thanks and blessings to all who have helped me here this night.

May there be peace and love between us whenever we meet again. So shall it be.

Life's Journey

No light is free of shadows,
For shadows reveal the light.
One cannot be without the other,
Just as day must have the night.
True spiritual power exists in balance
Within each being and affair.
But nothing is created perfect.
Perfection comes from work and care.
Our guides and guardians do their best
To help our journey day by day,
With words of wisdom and of love,
Whispered in their quiet way.
Angels of both light and shadow
Project to us great joy and bliss,
And every day renew our hopes
And keep us going with an angel kiss.

—D. J. Conway, 2008

Books of Interest

Abadie, M. J. *The Everything Angels Book*. Avon, MA: Adams
Media, 2000.

Andrews, Ted. *How to Meet & Work with Spirit Guides*. St. Paul,
MN: Llewellyn, 1992.

Barrett, Francis. *The Magus*. Secaucus, NJ: The Citadel Press,
1980.

Baskin, Wade. *Dictionary of Satanism*. New York: Philosophical
Library, 1962.

Belhayes, Iris, with Enid. *Spirit Guides*. San Diego, CA: ACS Publications, 1986.

Berkowitz, Rita S., and Deborah S. Romaine. *The Complete Idiot's Guide to Communicating with Spirits*. Indianapolis, IN: Alpha Books, 2002.

———. *Empowering Your Life with Angels*. Indianapolis, IN: Alpha Books, 2004.

Brown, Dan. *Angels & Demons*. New York: Pocket Books, 2000.

———. *The Da Vinci Code*. New York: Doubleday, 2003.

Browne, Sylvia. *Angels & Spirit Guides* (audiocassette). Carlsbad, CA: Hay House, 1999.

———. *Contacting Your Spirit Guide*. Carlsbad, CA: Hay House, 2005.

———. *The Other Side and Back*. New York: Dutton Books, 1999.

———. *Sylvia Browne's Book of Angels*. Carlsbad, CA: Hay House, 2003.

Bunson, Matthew. *Angels A to Z: A Who's Who of the Heavenly Host*. New York: Three Rivers Press, 1996.

Campbell, Joseph. *The Way of the Animal Powers*. San Francisco: Harper & Row, 1983.

Cirlot, J. E. *A Dictionary of Symbols*. Translated by Jack Sage. New York: Philosophical Library, 1971.

Conway, D. J. *Mystical Dragon Magick*. Woodbury, MN: Llewellyn, 2007.

Craughwell, Thomas J. *Saints for Every Occasion: 101 of Heaven's Most Powerful Patrons*. Charlotte, NC: Stampley Enterprises, 2001.

Daniel, Alma, Timothy Wyllie, and Andrew Ramer. *Ask Your Angels: A Practical Guide to Working with the Messengers of Heaven to Empower and Enrich Your Life*. New York: Ballantine, 1992.

Davidson, Gustav. *A Dictionary of Angels Including the Fallen Angels*. Reissue Edition. New York: The Free Press, 1994.

De Montfort, St. Louis. Translated by Fr. Frederick Faber. *True Devotion to Mary*. Rockford, IL: Tan Books and Publishers, 1941.

Dumars, Denise, and Lori Nyx. *The Dark Archetype: Exploring the Shadow Side of the Divine*. Franklin Lakes, NJ: New Page Books, 2003.

Eason, Cassandra. *The Illustrated Directory of Healing Crystals*. London: Collins & Brown, 2003.

Editors of Beliefnet. *The Big Book of Angels*. Emmaus, PA: Beliefnet/Rodale, 2002.

Farmer, David. *The Oxford Dictionary of Saints*. Oxford: Oxford University Press, 1997.

Fox, Sabrina. *Loved by Angels: Angels Are Right Beside Us Even If We Don't Yet See Them*. Nashville, TN: Bluestar Communication, 1999.

Garfield, Laeh Maggie, and Jack Grant. *Companions in Spirit*. Berkeley, CA: Celestial Arts, 1984.

Georgian, Linda. *Your Guardian Angels: Use the Power of Angelic Messengers to Enrich and Empower Your Life*. New York: Fireside, 1994.

Giovetti, Paola. Translated by Toby McCormick. *Angels: The Role of Celestial Guardians and Beings of Light*. York Beach, ME: Samuel Weiser, 1993.

Goddard, David. *The Sacred Magic of the Angels*. York Beach, ME: Samuel Weiser, 1996.

Godwin, Malcolm. *Angels: An Endangered Species*. New York: Simon & Schuster, 1990.

Guardini, Romano. *The Art of Praying*. Manchester, NH: Sophia Institute Press, 1985.

———. *The Rosary of Our Lady*. Manchester, NH: Sophia Institute Press, 1983.

Guiley, Rosemary Ellen. *The Encyclopedia of Angels*. New York: Checkmark Books, 2004.

———. *The Encyclopedia of Ghosts and Spirits*. New York: Facts on File, 1992.

Haldane, Albert, and Simha Seraya, with Barbara Lagowski. *Angel Signs*. San Francisco: HarperCollins, 2002.

Hall, Judy. *The Crystal Bible*. Cincinnati, OH: Walking Stick Press, 2004.

Hallam, Elizabeth, ed. *Saints: Who They Are and How They Help You*. New York: Simon & Schuster, 1994.

Hone, William, ed. Translated by Jeremiah Jones and William Wake. *The Lost Books of the Bible*. New York: Crown Publishers, 1979.

Howard, Michael. *Finding Your Guardian Angel Through Incense & Candle Burning*. San Francisco: Thorsons, 1991.

Jarry, Veronique. *Who Is Your Guardian Angel?* New York: Warner Books, 1998.

Johnson, K. Paul. *The Masters Revealed: Madame Blavatsky and the Myth of the Great White Lodge*. Albany, NY: State University of New York Press, 1994.

Johnson, Kevin Orlin. *Rosary: Mysteries, Meditations, and the Telling of the Beads*. Dallas, TX: Pangaeus Press, 1996.

Jones, Kathleen. *Women Saints: Lives of Faith and Courage*. Tunbridge Wells, UK: Burns & Oates, 1999.

Jupiter, Aryella. *The Great Encyclopedia of Angels*. Coral Springs, FL: Llumina Press, 2004.

La Plante, Alice, and Clare La Plante. *Heaven Help Us: The Worrier's Guide to the Patron Saints.* New York: Dell, 1999.

Laurence, Richard (translator). *The Book of Enoch the Prophet.* Kempton, IL: Adventures Unlimited Press, 2000. First published by William Clowes & Sons, London, 1883.

Layton, Bentley. *The Gnostic Scriptures.* Garden City, NY: Doubleday, 1987.

Lewis, James R., and Evelyn Dorothy Oliver. *Angels A to Z.* Canton, MI: Visible Ink Press, 1996.

Luckert, Karl W. *Egyptian Light and Hebrew Fire.* New York: State University of New York Press, 1991.

MacGregor, Trish. *The Everything Astrology Book.* Holbrook, MA: Adams Media Corporation, 1999.

Malbrough, Ray T. *Charms, Spells & Formulas.* St. Paul, MN: Llewellyn, 1986.

———. *The Magical Power of the Saints.* St. Paul, MN: Llewellyn, 1998.

Mark, Barbara, and Trudy Griswold. *Angelspeake: How to Talk with Your Angels.* New York: Simon & Schuster, 1995.

Mathers, S. Liddell MacGregor (translator). *The Greater Key of Solomon.* Chicago: The de Laurence Co., 1914.

McColman, Carl. *The Complete Idiot's Guide to Paganism.* Indianapolis, IN: Alpha Books, 2002.

McGerr, Angela. *An Angel for Every Day.* London: Quadrille Publishing, 2006.

Meyer, Marvin W. (translator). *The Secret Teachings of Jesus.* New York: Vintage Books, 1986.

Newhouse, Flower A. *The Kingdom of the Shining Ones.* Escondido, CA: The Christward Ministry, 1955.

————. *Rediscovering the Angels.* Escondido, CA: The Christward Ministry, 1976.

O'Neill, Kim. *How to Talk with Your Angels.* New York: Avon Books, 1995.

Pagels, Elaine. *The Gnostic Gospels.* New York: Random House, 1979.

————. *The Origin of Satan.* New York: Random House, 1995.

Penczak, Christopher. *Spirit Allies: Meet Your Team from the Other Side.* York Beach, ME: Weiser Books, 2002.

Picknett, Lynn. *The Secret History of Lucifer.* New York: Carroll & Graf Publishers, 2005.

Price, John Randolph. *Angel Energy: How to Harness the Power of Angels in Your Everyday Life.* New York: Fawcett Columbine, 1995.

————. *Angels Within Us: A Spiritual Guide to the Twenty-Two Angels That Govern Our Lives.* New York: Fawcett, 1993.

Prophet, Elizabeth Clare. *Fallen Angels and the Origins of Evil.* Corwin Springs, MT: Summit University Press, 2000.

Raven, Hazel. *The Angel Bible: The Definitive Guide to Angel Wisdom.* New York: Sterling Publishing, 2006.

Robinson, James M, ed. *The Nag Hammadi Library.* Reprint. New York: Harper & Row, 1981.

Ronner, John. *Do You Have a Guardian Angel?* Murfreeboro, TN: Mamre Press, 1985.

————. *Know Your Angels.* Murfreeboro, TN: Mamre Press, 1993.

Sandoval, Annette. *The Directory of Saints: A Concise Guide to Patron Saints.* New York: Signet/Penguin, 1997.

Sargent, Denny. *Your Guardian Angel and You.* York Beach, ME: Weiser Books, 2004.

Simmons, Robert, and Naisha Ahsian. *The Book of Stones.* East Montpelier, VT: Heaven & Earth Publishing, 2005.

Smith, Morton. *The Secret Gospel.* London: Gollancz, 1973.

Spretnak, Charlene. *Missing Mary.* New York: Palgrave Macmillan, 2004.

Stein, Diane. *Psychic Healing with Spirit Guides and Angels.* Freedom, CA: The Crossing Press, 1996.

Steiner, Rudolf. *Guardian Angels: Connecting with Our Spiritual Guides and Helpers.* Forest Row, UK: Rudolf Steiner Press, 2004.

Stone, Joshua David. *The Ascended Masters Light the Way.* Sedona, AZ: Light Technology Publishing, 1995.

Taylor, Terry Lynn. *The Angel Experience.* San Rafael, CA: Amber-Allen Publishing, 1998.

———. *Messengers of Light.* Tiburon, CA: New World Library, 1990.

———. *Messengers of Love, Light & Grace.* Novato, CA: New World Library, 2005.

Turner, Alice K. *The History of Hell.* New York: Harcourt Brace, 1993.

Virtue, Doreen. *Angel Guidance Board.* Carlsbad, CA: Hay House, 2005.

———. *Angel Medicine.* Carlsbad, CA: Hay House, 2004.

———. *Angels 101.* Carlsbad, CA: Hay House, 2006.

———. *Archangels and Ascended Masters: A Guide to Working and Healing with Divinities and Deities.* Carlsbad, CA: Hay House, 2003.

———. *Connecting with Your Angels Kit.* Carlsbad, CA: Hay House, 2004.

———. *Earth Angels*. Carlsbad, CA: Hay House, 2002.

———. *Fairies 101*. Carlsbad, CA: Hay House, 2007.

———. *Goddesses and Angels*. Carlsbad, CA: Hay House, 2005.

———. *Healing with the Angels: How the Angels Can Assist You in Every Area of Your Life*. Carlsbad, CA: Hay House, 1999.

———. *Messages from Your Angels: What Your Angels Want You to Know*. Carlsbad, CA: Hay House, 2003.

Virtue, Doreen, with Judith Lukomski. *Crystal Therapy: How to Heal and Empower Your Life with Crystal Energy*. Carlsbad, CA: Hay House, 2005.

Walsh-Roberts, Paul D. *From Atoms to Angels: The Spiritual Forces Shaping Your Life*. Dublin, Ireland: Gateway, 2000.

Wang, Robert. *The Qabalistic Tarot*. York Beach, ME: Samuel Weiser, 1983.

Webster, Richard. *Practical Guide to Past-Life Memories: Twelve Proven Methods*. St. Paul, MN: Llewellyn, 2001.

———. *Praying with Angels*. Woodbury, MN: Llewellyn, 2007.

———. *Spirit Guides & Angel Guardians: Contact Your Invisible Helpers*. St. Paul, MN: Llewellyn, 1998.

White, Ruth. *Working with Spirit Guides*. London: Piatkus, 2004.

———. *Working with Your Guides and Angels*. Boston: Weiser Books, 1997.

A native of the Pacific Northwest, author D. J. Conway has made the occult fields her lifelong quest and study. Her search for knowledge has covered every aspect of Paganism and Wicca to New Age and Eastern philosophies, history, customs, mythologies, and folklore. In 1998, she was voted Best Wiccan and New Age Author by *Silver Chalice*, a Pagan magazine. She was awarded the Prolific Pagans Award for Excellence and the *Earthsongs* Readers' Choice Award. D. J. also tied for second place in the 2006 COVR Visionary Awards. She lives a rather quiet life with her family, friends, and fur people, with most of her time spent researching and writing.

She is a member of the Silver and Gold Crown Society, the Black Hat Society, and she is a Dragon Mystic.

Please visit her website, www.djconway.com.

Many of Llewellyn's authors have websites with additional information and resources. For more information, please visit our website at http://www.llewellyn.com.

Mystical Dragon Magick
Teachings of the Five Inner Rings

D. J. CONWAY

Dragons have been sharing their power with humanity throughout history and across cultures. These magickal creatures can strengthen your spellwork and guide you to new realms of consciousness.

D. J. Conway's sequel to *Dancing with Dragons* takes dragon magick to the highest level. Discover how to attract dragons, draw on their legendary energy and wisdom, and partner with them as co-magicians. Each of the five "Inner Rings"—apprentice, enchanter, shaman, warrior, and mystic—introduces new methods for working dragon magick and guides you to a higher path of spiritual consciousness. From shape shifting to herbal spells, this guide to dragon magick also offers plenty of practical methods for working with these otherworldly creatures.

ISBN: 978–0-7387-1099-0
264 pages $18.95

Dancing with Dragons

Invoke Their Ageless Wisdom & Power

D. J. CONWAY

Access one of the most potent life forces in the astral universe: the wise and magickal dragon. Dragons do exist! They inhabit the astral plane that interpenetrates our physical world. Now, *Dancing with Dragons* makes the vast and wonderful hoard of dragon power available to you. Learn to call, befriend, and utilize the wisdom of these mythical creatures for increased spiritual fulfillment, knowledge, health, and happiness.

Dancing with dragons is a joyful experience. Whether you are a practicing magician, a devotee of role-playing games, or a seeker looking to tap the dragon's vast astral power, this book will help you forge a magickal partnership with these magnificent astral creatures.

ISBN: 978-1-56718-165-4

320 pages $18.95

To order, call 1-877-NEW-WRLD
Prices subject to change without notice
Order at Llewellyn.com 24 hours a day, 7 days a week!

Azrael Loves Chocolate, Michael's a Jock

An Insider's Guide to What Your Angels Are Really Like

CHANTEL LYSETTE

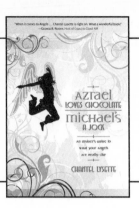

Relating to the angels isn't always easy for us lowly humans. So, angel intuitive Chantel Lysette found a way to bring "Mike," "Gabe," and their divine gang down to earth. Irreverent and uplifting, this book will help you understand and connect with these celestial beings who—like any close friend—want to hear from you.

With humor and sass, Lysette interviews twelve archangels and reveals their likes, dislikes, hobbies, and more. Michael loves to pull pranks; Sandalphon grooves on jazz; and Azrael, the angel of death, has a sweet tooth. Tag along with Lysette as she chats with each heavenly host and visits their celestial mansions. Discover what the angels think of each other, how they view humankind, and when each one is most likely to show up in your life.

Breaking the ice between humanity and divinity, this unique guide to the angels will inspire you to get off your butt and develop a personal relationship with your spiritual teachers.

> *"Whatever you say about the tallest angel in Heaven, it had better be nice."*
> —Archangel Michael, speaking about Metatron

ISBN: 978-0-7387-1441-7

240 pages $14.95